VEGAN À LA MODE

More Than 100 Frozen Treats for Every Day of the Year

HANNAH KAMINSKY

Skyhorse Publishing

Skyhorse Publishing books may be purchased in bulk at special discounts for sales promotion, corporate gifts, fund-raising, or educational purposes. Special editions can also be created to specifications. For details, contact the Special Sales Department, Skyhorse Publishing, 307 West 36th Street, 11th Floor, New York, NY 10018 or info@skyhorsepublishing.com.

Skyhorse® and Skyhorse Publishing® are registered trademarks of Skyhorse Publishing, Inc.®, a Delaware corporation.

Visit our website at www.skyhorsepublishing.com.

10 9 8 7 6 5 4 3 2 1

Library of Congress Cataloging-in-Publication Data is available on file.

ISBN: 978-1-61608-724-1

Printed in China

TABLE OF CONTENTS

ACKNOWLEDGMENTS

Thanks are due to many people for making this book possible, including all of my thoughtful, supportive blog readers, and especially my mom and dad. Without their endless patience, expert dish washing, and tireless enthusiasm, my penchant for churning out frozen desserts would likely result in little more than an overstuffed freezer.

I'm also indebted to the brave and open-minded recipe testers who helped verify even my wildest recipes as accurate, easy to follow, and above all else, delicious. Those who lent their time, taste buds, and freezer space to the cause were Jenni Mischel, Amanda Crow, Sophia Magnone, Lisa Pitman, Lori, Dawn Hodose, Cat DiStasio, and Ted Lai.

Dishes provided for photography by Steelite on pages (18, 56, 164, 206, 208)

INTRODUCTION

If ever there was one dessert that could capture my heart, ice cream would be first in line, flowers and love letters in hand. From an early age, the attraction was undeniable. A forbidden, rare pleasure at first, reserved only for birthdays and holidays, the chance to enjoy ice cream again elevated any event into a day worth waiting for. Be it a generous scoop melting over the tender crumbs of a layer cake or a glassful topped off with a bubbly swig of root beer, that sweet, creamy treat never got old. Unadventurous at first, vanilla, chocolate, and mint chocolate chip were the only flavors acceptable until that fateful trip to Italy as a teenager. Artful mounds of gelato in every color of the rainbow glittered behind frosted glass cases, luring me to taste a new world of possibilities. Rose petal gelato, scooping out as a lovely shade of pink blush—what girl could resist? How about salted caramel? Cinnamon? Just as suddenly as ice cream had become an acceptable daily affair, the sky was the limit for new taste sensations.

Never ceasing to pair flavors and dream up new ideas, my frozen dessert experiments grew only more daring over time. The best part about making your own ice cream, other than being able to control the quality of the ingredients, is having the freedom to mix up exactly the blend you crave. Toss peanuts into your chocolate fudge if you wish, take out a caramel ripple and add toffee pieces instead—let your sweet tooth call the shots and go wild! Approach the following recipes with an open mind and curious palate for the best results.

What's in a name?

Ice cream, gelato, frozen custard, ice milk, sherbet, sorbet—deep down in the core of their frozen hearts, what is it that separates these distinct varieties of frozen desserts? At the end of the day, it all comes down to butterfat. Typically, the fattier the concoction, the richer the end results, beginning with frozen custard and moving down to the lightest of the batch, sorbet, that never includes dairy at all. Those minute differences become far more difficult to define when talking about vegan frozen treats, containing none of the telltale dairy component. For the purposes of keeping things nice and simple, no overwrought fancy terms needed, I refer to anything creamy or made with non-dairy milk as "ice cream," and anything with a fruit or vegetable base as "sorbet."

INGREDIENTS GLOSSARY

Agave Nectar

Derived from the same plant as tequila but far less potent, agave is the sweet syrup at the core of cacti. It is available in both light and dark varieties; the dark possesses a more nuanced, complex, and somewhat floral flavor, while the light tends to provide only a clean sweetness. Unrefined, agave nectar has a much lower glycemic index than many traditional granulated sweeteners, and is therefore consumed by some diabetics in moderation. Any health food or natural food store worth its stuff should readily stock agave nectar.

Agar

Known also as agar agar or kanten, agar is a gelatinous substance made out of seaweed. It is a perfect substitute for traditional gelatin, which is extracted from the collagen of animals' connective tissues and obviously extremely not vegan. Agar comes in both powdered and flaked form. I prefer to use the powder because it is easier to incorporate smoothly into puddings, faster to thicken, and measures gram for gram like standard gelatin. However, if you can only find the flakes, just whiz them in a spice grinder for a few minutes and, voilà! instant agar powder! Agar can be found in Asian markets and some health food stores.

All-Purpose Gluten-Free Flour Blend

Standard sorbet and ice cream bases are naturally gluten-free, but some of the fancier recipes call for baked goods to be mixed or blended in. It's easy enough to switch out the wheat flour for a more allergy-friendly mix, though. Many ready-made combinations of gluten-free flours exist in the marketplace now, and though there are varying results based on the brand and the exact blend, most can replicate the texture of standard flour fairly well. My top pick is made by Bob's Red Mill, which can be substituted 1:1 for all-purpose flour. If you'd like to whip up your own blend, that's also easy enough as long as you have a well-stocked pantry.

All-Purpose Gluten-Free Flour Blend
6 Cups White Rice Flour
2 Cups Potato Starch or Cornstarch
1 Cup Tapioca Flour
2 Tablespoons Xanthan Gum

Simply whisk all of the dry goods together until thoroughly mixed. Store in an airtight container, and measure out as needed. If the recipe you're following already calls for xanthan gum, you can omit it from this blend.

All-Purpose Flour

While wonderful flours can be made from all sorts of grains, beans, nuts, and seeds, the gold standard in everyday baking would be all-purpose. Falling somewhere between cake flour and bread flour, all-purpose flour has the ability to create light desserts which still have substance. It is therefore used most often in my recipes, and stocked as one of my pantry staples. All-purpose flour may be labeled in stores as unbleached white flour or simply "plain flour."

Almond Meal/Flour

Almond flour is simply the end result of grinding down raw almonds into a fine powder; almond meal is generally just a bit coarser. To make your own, just throw a pound or so of completely unadulterated almonds into your food processor, and let the machine work its magic. If you opt to stock up and save some for later, be sure to store the freshly ground almond flour in an airtight container in the refrigerator or freezer. Due to their high oil content, ground nuts can go rancid fairly quickly. To cut down on labor and save a little time, almond flour or meal can be purchased in bulk from natural food grocers.

Alum

A throwback to the olden days of food preservation, alum is mainly used for pickling fruits and vegetables, and to keep foods crisp in texture and fresh in taste. Still available right next to the allspice in all major grocery stores, it's a potent salt (like sodium or potassium) which must always be used sparingly, as it can prove toxic if ingested in large doses (over 1 ounce at a time). If the sound of that makes you nervous, feel free to omit the alum when called for. It carries a certain astringent, acidic taste that's hard to describe, but you won't miss it too much if you've never used it in the first place.

Apple Cider Vinegar

As with oil, vinegar can be made from all sorts of fruits, grains, and roots, which all create unique flavor profiles and chemical compositions in the finished product. Thinking along these lines, apple cider vinegar could be considered the olive oil of vinegars—flavorful, useful, and an all-around great thing to have on hand. Regular white wine vinegar or the other standard options would certainly *work,* but the distinctive "twang" of apple cider vinegar rounds out baked goods so perfectly, and it is so easy to find . . . why wouldn't you use it? Hunt around the oil and salad dressing aisles in your local supermarket, where you should have no problem securing a bottle.

Arrowroot Powder/Flour

Thanks to arrowroot, you can thicken sauces, puddings, and mousses with ease. This white powder is very similar to kudzu and is often compared to other starchy flours. However, arrowroot is so fine that it produces much smoother, creamier results, and is less likely to stick together and form large, glutinous lumps. It freezes very nicely, which is why it's one of my favorite thickeners when making ice cream. Most mega marts have one or two brands to choose from tucked in among the flours in the baking aisle.

Barley Malt Syrup

A dark brown, thick syrup bearing the distinctive aroma of toasted cereal, barley malt syrup is about half as sweet as sugar, but at least ten times as flavorful. Dark and wholesome, it's an excellent alternative to molasses. Being so sticky, it's a bit trickier to use than the ubiquitous malted milk powder, but contributes a much fuller flavor in my opinion. Many standard grocery stores now carry it in the natural ingredient section, and no health food store worth its salt would be caught without at least a jar or two on hand.

Black Cocoa Powder

What do you get when you oxidize Dutch-processed cocoa powder to the extreme? Black cocoa, of course! Dark as coal, it certainly lives up to its name and produces amazing, jet-black color in baked goods. However, it has a much lower fat content than standard cocoa, and should therefore be used sparingly to avoid altering the texture of your baked goods. I rarely use black cocoa, because it is difficult to find and more expensive than the alternative. Nonetheless, if you wish to create breathtaking chocolate desserts, black cocoa will never fail to impress. You can hunt it down at some tea or spice specialty shops, but if all else fails, a search online should prove fruitful. Feel free to substitute regular Dutch-processed cocoa for an equally tasty, if comparatively pale, dessert.

Brown Rice Syrup

Caramel-colored and thick like honey, brown rice syrup is a natural sweetener that is produced via the fermentation of brown rice. It is actually less sweet than granulated sugar, adding a wholesome complexity to baked goods. The deep flavor of brown rice syrup is best cast in supporting roles, complementing other aspects of the dish without taking center stage. Brown rice syrup can be found in health food stores across the map, but corn syrup will make a suitable substitute, if you are unable to find it locally.

Cacao Nibs

Also known as raw chocolate, cacao nibs are unprocessed cacao nuts, simply broken up into smaller pieces. Much more bitter and harsh than the sweet, mellow chocolate found in bars or chips, it is often used for texture and accent flavor in most desserts. Sometimes it can be found coated in sugar to soften its inherent acidity, but for baking, you want the plain, raw version if possible. Seek out bags of cacao nibs in health food stores; if you're really lucky, you may be able to find them in the bulk bins of well-stocked specialty stores.

Chocolate (Semi-Sweet and Bittersweet)

Chocolate is chocolate, right? One would assume so, but many name brands that prefer quantity to quality would beg to differ. Obviously milk chocolate is out of the picture, yet some dark and semi-sweet chocolates still don't make the vegan cut. Even those that claim to be "70% cacao solids, extra-special dark" may have milk solids or butterfat lurking within. Don't buy the hype or the filler! Stay vigilant and check labels for milk-based ingredients, as unadulterated chocolate is far superior. Semi-sweet has approximately half as much sugar as cocoa solids, and bittersweet tends to have even less.

Chocolate Crème-Filled Sandwich Cookies

As America's favorite cookie, it is no surprise that the Oreo® would come up sooner or later on this list. While the original Oreo is now changing its ways to take out the trans-fats and animal products, there are many other options that are even more ethically acceptable. Newman's Own® makes an excellent organic version that tastes just like the cookies you might remember from your childhood. Plus, along with some exciting flavor variations, Newman-O's (as they are called) can even be found in a wheat-free format! Any Oreo-like cocoa wafers with a vegan crème filling will do, so it is up to your own discretion as to which brand you would like to endorse.

Coconut Milk

When called for in this book, I'm referring to regular, full-fat coconut milk. In the case of ice cream, light coconut milk cannot be substituted without detrimental effects to the final texture. That fat is necessary for a smooth, creamy mouth feel, and of course a richer taste. Plain coconut milk is found canned in the ethnic foods aisle of the grocery store. You can make it yourself from fresh coconut meat, but in most baking and general dessert-making cases, when it's not the featured flavor, the added hassle honestly isn't worth the expense or effort.

Cocoa Butter

Chocolate is comprised of two key elements: The cocoa solids, which give it that distinct cocoa flavor, and the cocoa butter, which is the fat that provides the body. Cocoa butter is solid at room temperate like all tropical oils, so it's best to always measure it after melting, as the firm chunks can appear deceptively voluminous. For making your own white chocolate (page 225), it's really important to pick up high-quality, food-grade cocoa butter, since that's the main ingredient that you're going to taste. As a popular ingredient in body lotions and lip balms, some offerings come with fillers and undesirable additives, so shop carefully if you search locally. Also avoid deodorized cocoa butter, unless you prefer taste-free food.

Confectioner's Sugar

Otherwise known as powdered sugar, icing sugar, or 10x sugar, confectioner's sugar is a very finely ground version of standard white sugar, often with a touch of starch included to prevent clumping. There are many vegan options on the market, so just keep your eyes open and you will likely find a good supply. You can make your own confectioner's sugar by powdering 1 cup of granulated sugar with 1 tablespoon of cornstarch in your food processor or spice grinder. Simply blend the sugar and cornstarch on the highest speed for about two minutes, allowing the dust to settle before opening your machine up—unless you want to inhale a cloud of sugar!

Flavor Extracts

In most cases, I try to stay as far away from extracts as possible, because they are all too often artificial, insipid, and a poor replacement for the real thing. However, real vanilla and almond are my two main exceptions, as high-quality extracts from the actual sources are readily available in most markets. Just make sure to avoid any bottles that contain sugar, corn syrup, colors, or chemical stabilizers in addition to your flavor of choice. For some of the more unusual extracts, if your supermarket searches end up unsuccessful, the Internet will never let you down.

Flax Seeds

Ground flax seeds make an excellent vegan egg-replacer when combined with water. One tablespoon of the whole seeds produces approximately 1½ tablespoons of the ground powder. While you can purchase preground flax meal in many stores, I prefer to grind the flax seeds fresh for each recipe, as they tend to go rancid rather quickly once broken down. Not to mention, it takes mere seconds to powder your own flax seeds in a spice grinder! If you do opt to purchase flax meal instead, be sure to store the powder in your refrigerator or freezer until you are ready to use it. These tiny seeds can be found in bulk bins and prepackaged in the baking aisle of natural food stores.

Garbanzo (Chickpea) Flour

Gaining popularity as a versatile, gluten-free flour, garbanzo flour is just as you might imagine: nothing but dried, ground chickpeas! Although it is now used primarily in baking to substitute for wheat flours and to add a certain density to cakes or cookies, it can also be cooked with water like polenta, and eaten either as a hot porridge or let set overnight in a baking dish, sliced, and then fried to make what is called chickpea panisse. Just be warned that eaten raw (if, say, someone decided to sample raw cookie batter that contains garbanzo flour) it is very bitter and unpleasant.

Garbanzo flour should be readily available in most grocery stores in the baking or natural foods section, but if you have a powerful blender like a VitaMix® (see Kitchen Toys and Tools) with a dry grinding container, you can make your own from dried, split chickpeas (also known as chana dal). Process 2 cups of legumes at a time, and use the plunger to keep things moving. Once finely ground, let the mixture sit for a few minutes before removing the lid of the container, so that the dust can settle.

Graham Crackers and Graham Cracker Crumbs

When I first went searching for vegan graham crackers, I was appalled by my lack of options. Why every brand in sight needed to include honey was beyond me. So, what is a hungry vegan baker to do in a tight situation like this? Keep on looking, of course. Concealed amongst the rest, and often in natural foods stores, there are a few brands that exclude all animal products. You can of course make your own and avoid a wild goose chase, following the recipe on page 203. Once you secure your crackers, you have two options to turn them into crumbs. For a coarse, more varied crumb, toss them into a sturdy plastic bag and just go at it with a rubber mallet or rolling pin. To achieve a fine, even crumb, grind them down in your food processor or spice grinder in batches, and you will have a perfect powder in no time.

Granulated Sugar

Yes, plain old, regular white sugar. Surprised to see this basic sweetener here? It's true that all sugar (beet or cane) is derived from plant sources and therefore vegan by nature. However, there are some sneaky things going on behind the scenes in big corporations these days. Some cane sugar is filtered using bone char, a very nonvegan process, but it will never be specified on any labels. If you're not sure about the brand that you typically buy, your best bet is to contact the manufacturer directly and ask.

To bypass this problem, many vegans purchase unbleached cane sugar. While it is a suitable substitute, unbleached cane sugar does have a higher molasses content than white sugar, so it has more of a brown sugar-like flavor, and tends to produce desserts that are denser. Luckily, there are a few caring companies that go through great pains to ensure the purity of their sugar products, such as Florida Crystals® and Amalgamated Sugar Company®, the suppliers to White Satin, Fred Meyer, Western Family, and Parade. I typically opt for one of these vegan sugar brands to get the best results. You can often find appropriate sugar in health food store bulk bins these days to save some money, but as always, verify the source before forking over the cash. As sugar can be a touchy vegan subject, it is best to use your own judgment when considering which brand to purchase.

Instant Coffee Powder

Though completely unfit for drinking as intended, instant coffee powder is an ideal way to add those crave-worthy roasted, smoky notes to any dessert without also incorporating a lot of extra liquid. This is especially important when keeping ratios intact for ice cream. Stored in the fridge, a small jar should last a long time. You can even find decaf versions, in case you're more sensitive to caffeine but still want that flavor in your recipes. I prefer powder to granules because they dissolve more easily, but both can work interchangeably with a bit of vigorous mixing.

Maple Syrup

One of my absolute favorite sweeteners, there is simply no substitute for real, 100 percent maple syrup. The flavor is like nothing else out there, and I have yet to meet a single brand of pancake syrup that could even come close. Of course, this incredible indulgence does come at a hefty price, and the costs only continue to rise as the years go by. Though it would be absolute sacrilege to use anything but authentic grade-B maple syrup on pancakes or waffles in my house, I will sometimes bend the rules in recipes where it isn't such a prominent flavor, in order to save some money. In these instances, I'll substitute with a maple-agave blend, which still carries the flavor from the actual source, but bulks it up with an equal dose of agave for sweetening power.

Maraschino Cherries

Ghastly red marbles that bear only a passing resemblance to the fresh fruits they once were, maraschino cherries are generally an ingredient I avoid at all costs. However, for the sake of nostalgia and preserving the integrity of certain classic flavor combinations, I have been known to make a few exceptions. What I take issue with most is the intense (and vaguely bitter) artificial coloring and syrupy sweetness, typically contributed by high-fructose corn syrup. Thankfully, with a bit of hunting, you can find natural alternatives out there. Versions produced by Luxardo®, Silver Palate®, and Tillen Farms®, for example, contain no preservatives and are colored solely by fruit and vegetable extracts. They can be found in specialty grocery stores and online.

Marshmallows

Snow-white, fluffy pillows of sugar, it's no secret that these simple treats are one of my favorite confections. Most hold a dirty little secret of their own though; the average mallow is made from gelatin, which is made from the collagen in animals' skin and bones. Truly gruesome stuff for such innocent candy! Luckily, there are now two vegan options on the market that far surpass the original inspirations, if you ask me. Dandies by Chicago Soy Dairy are similar to a jet-puffed variety, while Sweet and Sara makes a square mallow with a more handmade appearance. Both will make a marshmallow lover like myself exceedingly happy, and can be found in most Whole Foods Markets.

Matcha/Maccha Powder

Perhaps one of my all-time favorite flavorings, matcha is a very high-quality, powdered green tea. It is used primarily in Japanese tea ceremonies and can have an intense, complex, and bitter taste when used in large amounts. Contrary to what many new bakers think, this is NOT the same as the green tea leaves you'll find in mega-mart tea bags! Those are vastly inferior in the flavor department, and real matcha is ground much finer. There are many levels of quality, with each step up in grade carrying a higher price tag. Because it can become quite pricey, I would suggest buying a medium grade, which should be readily available at any specialty tea store. When translated directly from Japanese, the spelling is "maccha," but the typical English spelling is matcha. Whichever way the package is labeled, you will still find green tea powder within.

Non-Dairy Margarine

It is a basic kitchen staple at its core, but good margarine can actually be quite elusive if you do not know what to look for. Some name brands contain whey or other milk-derivatives, while others conceal the elusive, animal-derived vitamin D3, so be alert when scanning ingredient labels. For ease, I prefer to use stick margarines, such as Earth Balance® or Willow Run®. Never try to substitute spreadable margarine from a tub! These varieties have much more water to allow them to spread while cold, and will thus bake differently. I always use unsalted margarine unless otherwise noted, but you are welcome to use salted as long as you remove about ¼ teaspoon of salt from the recipe. Overly salted food is one of the first flaws that diners pick up on, so take care with your seasoning!

Non-Dairy Milk

The foundation of all ice cream recipes, I kept this critical ingredient somewhat ambiguous for a reason. Most types of non-dairy milk will work in these recipes, and I wouldn't want to limit anyone with specific allergies. The only type that I absolutely *do not* recommend using is rice milk, as it tends to be much thinner, often gritty, and completely lacking in the body necessary to make rich, satisfying frozen desserts. Unless explicitly specified, any other type of vegan milk-substitute will work. My top pick for ice cream making is unsweetened almond milk because it tends to be a bit thicker, richer, and still has a neutral flavor. For a deluxe version of any recipe, with the most luxurious, rich texture possible, spring for plain vegan creamer (soy- or coconut-based) instead. Don't be afraid to experiment, though; there's a lot to choose from!

Nutritional Yeast

Unlike active yeast, nutritional yeast is not used to leaven baked goods, but to flavor all sorts of dishes. Prized for its distinctly savory, cheesy flavor, it's a staple in most vegan pantries and is finally starting to gain recognition in mainstream cooking as well. Though almost always found in savory recipes, I sometimes like to add a tiny pinch to particular desserts, bringing out its more subtle buttery characteristics. There is no substitute for nutritional yeast, so if you can't find it, your best bet here is to simply leave it out.

Orange Blossom Water

Distilled from bitter-orange flowers, this delicately perfumed extract isn't citrus-flavored as it might sound, but floral. A little bit goes a long way, so even a small bottle should last you a good, long time. Middle Eastern markets are your best bet for reasonably priced options. In a pinch, rose water can work instead.

Phyllo Dough

Alternately spelled "fillo" or "filo" dough, this gossamer-thin pastry is not something for the average cook (or even most highly skilled ones) to attempt at home. Rather, it's much more sensible to buy it frozen at the grocery store, where most brands should be vegan. Just double-check labels for any sneaky dairy derivatives that may be lurking, and all the rest should be good.

Red Wine

While I don't actually drink, I can tell you that if your wine isn't something you'd want in a glass, it's not something you'd want in a cake or sorbet, either. Avoid so-called cooking wines and just go with something moderately priced, and on the sweeter side to complement the dessert that it's going into. Don't be afraid to ask for help when you go shopping; the people who work at wine stores tend to have good advice about these things! Be vigilant and do your homework though, because not all wines are vegan. Shockingly, some are filtered through isinglass, which is actually made from fish bladders! So, to avoid a fishy brew, double check brands on http://www.barnivore.com/wine.

Ricemellow Crème®

Remember that old childhood favorite, Marshmallow Fluff®? Well, Ricemellow Crème is its vegan equivalent, devoid of animal-based gelatins and refined sugars. Light, fluffy, and unlike anything else currently on the market, I have yet to find a suitable vegan alternative for Ricemellow Crème. It can be purchased at most natural food stores, or via online purveyors.

Salt

The importance of salt in desserts cannot be overstated, especially when it comes to ice cream. It's that spark that makes flavors pop and balances out a bit of the sweetness that might otherwise overwhelm the palate. It also acts like sugar, helping to prevent large ice crystals and keeping your frozen treats at a scoopable consistency. In short, you do not want to leave this unassuming but critical ingredient out! Unless otherwise noted, I use regular old table salt (finely ground) in baking. Kosher salt can be fun to sprinkle directly over finished scoops before serving for an extra punch of flavor, but be careful not to overdo it; there's a fine line between salted and downright salty.

Soy (or Coconut) Creamer

Vegan creamer based on soy or coconut is a thicker liquid than regular non-dairy milk, though it is not an equal substitute for dairy-based heavy cream. While it adds richness and moisture to cakes and creamy spreads, vegan creamers lack the proper ratio of proteins necessary to make whipped cream. Rather, they consist primarily of sugars, and consequently boast a sweeter taste. Soy and coconut creamers are available in a number of flavors, all of which may be used for some additional flavoring, if desired. In a pinch, regular soy milk or other milk alternatives can be substituted, although the end results might not be quite as rich and thick.

Sprinkles

What's an ice cream sundae without a generous handful of sprinkles on top? Though these colorful toppers are made primarily of edible wax, they are often coated in confectioner's glaze, which is code for mashed-up insects, to give them their lustrous shine. Happily, you can now find specifically vegan sprinkles (sold as "sprinkelz") produced by the Let's Do . . .® company, in both chocolate and colored versions, which can be found at just about any health food store. You can also make your own; see page 212.

Tahini

An irreplaceable staple in Middle Eastern cuisine, most regular grocery stores should be able to accommodate your tahini requests. Tahini is a paste very much like peanut butter, but made from sesame seeds rather than nuts. If you don't have any on hand and a trip to the market is not in your immediate plans, then any other nut butter will provide exactly the same texture within a recipe, though it will impart a different overall taste. You can also make your own just as you would make nut butter, but a high-speed blender is highly recommended to achieve a smooth texture.

Tofu

Yes, I make desserts with tofu and I'm not ashamed to admit it! When I use tofu for baked goods and ice creams, I always reach for the aseptic, shelf-stable packs. Not only do they seem to last forever when unopened, but they also blend down into a perfectly smooth liquid when processed thoroughly, with not a trace of grit or off-flavors to be found. The most common brand is Mori-Nu, which is found all over the place, especially in Japanese and natural food stores, so just keep an eye peeled and you should have no problem locating it.

Turbinado Sugar

Coarse, light brown granulated sugar, I just love the sparkle that this edible glitter lends when applied to the outside of cookies. Though it's not the best choice for actually baking with since the large crystals make for an uneven distribution of sweetness, it adds a satisfying crunch and eye-appeal when used as decoration. Turbinado sugar is very easy to find in the baking department of any typical grocery store or mega mart.

Vanilla (Extract, Paste, and Beans)

One of the most important ingredients in a baker's arsenal, vanilla is found in countless forms and qualities. It goes without saying that artificial flavorings pale in comparison to the real thing. Madagascar vanilla is the traditional full-bodied vanilla that most people tend to appreciate in desserts, so stick with that and you can't go wrong. Happily, it's also the most common and moderately priced variety. To take your desserts up a step, vanilla paste brings in the same amount of flavor, but includes those lovely little vanilla bean flecks that make everyone think you busted out the good stuff and used whole beans. Vanilla paste can be substituted 1:1 for vanilla extract. Like whole vanilla beans, save the paste for things where you'll really see those specks of vanilla goodness, like ice creams, custards, and frostings. Vanilla beans, the most costly but flavorful and authentic option, can be used instead, at about 1 bean per 2 teaspoons of extract or paste.

Once you've split and scraped out the insides, don't toss that vanilla pod! Get the most for your money by stashing it in a container of granulated sugar, to slowly infuse the sugar with delicious vanilla flavor. Alternately, just store the pod in a container until it dries out, and then grind it up very finely in a high-speed blender and use it to augment a good vanilla extract. The flavor won't be nearly as strong as the seeds, but it does contribute to the illusion that you've used the good stuff.

Vegan "Cream Cheese"

Amazingly, many innovative companies now make dairy-free products that will give you the most authentic cream cheese frostings imaginable. These "cheeses" also hold up beautifully in cookie dough and pie crusts, contributing a great tangy flavor and excellent structure. My favorite brand is the classic Tofutti®, but there are now numerous options available that all work just as well in dessert applications. This ingredient is hard to replace with homemade varieties when seeking smooth, consistent ice creams, so I suggest that you check out your local mega mart or natural food grocer, or head online if all else fails.

Vegan "Sour Cream"

Another creative alternative comes to the rescue of vegan bakers everywhere! Vegan "sour cream" provides an amazingly similar, yet dairy-free version of the original tangy spread. In a pinch, I suppose you might be able to get away

KITCHEN TOOLS AND TOYS

The specific demands of ice cream making require some specialized tools that might not be considered standard kitchen equipment by everyone. Fear not—most are simple and inexpensive implements that are readily available at stores that sell kitchenware, and exhaustive searches of specialty stores shouldn't be necessary. Since the process of creating ice creams is so simple, attention to detail is key, which includes proper collection and care of your appliances, both big and small.

Blender

Having enough horsepower behind your blade can make the difference between silky-smooth custard and a grainy, chunky mess. A basic model can certainly work, as long as you give your mixtures plenty of time to purée, stopping to check the consistency frequently and scrape down the sides of the container to ensure that everything is getting to the blade. Always plan on straining your purées afterward, since there will inevitably be something or other left behind.

Given an unlimited budget, a high-speed blender is definitely what you want to buy, and I'm a big fan of my Vitamix®. Nothing breaks down food faster or smoother at that price point, and they're a snap to clean out when it's all over. The Blend Tec® is also a highly worthy option to investigate, for approximately the same cost.

Freezer

Everyone has one, but few people give it the attention it deserves. Water freezes at 32 degrees Fahrenheit, but a healthy freezer should hover closer to 0–5 degrees cold. This is critical for proper ice cream storage, because frozen desserts won't properly set up at warmer temperatures, and freeze into solid bricks if we're looking at sub-zero readings. If a thermometer isn't already built in to your particular appliance, it's worthwhile to invest in a simple dial-type model for approximately $2 at most hardware stores. You can get fancier versions that have digital readouts and alarms to let you know about serious temperature variations, but such bells and whistles are completely unnecessary.

Keep an eye out for excessive frost and ice coating the sides of your freezer, because that's a sign of an insufficient door seal. The air from outside is finding a way in due to a faulty closure, and sticking to the insides, turning into that coating of ice crystals. For the proper storage of anything, beyond just frozen desserts, this issue should be looked at by a professional and repaired immediately. A poor seal also means that the temperature is likely not at the level it should be, which is downright unsafe for long-term food storage.

Ice Cream Machines

The single most critical item required for making your frosty treats, aside from the freezer itself, is the ice cream machine. Once a prohibitively expensive luxury item, both unwieldy to use and incapable of churning out any decent amount of ice cream, it's a whole new world of frozen dessert technology out there now. Making ice cream at home has never been easier or more accessible, with countless options to delight your inner gadget geek. Originally limited to different sizes of hand-cranked wooden buckets, you can now find machines that will mix the base, chill themselves, churn the ice cream, do your taxes, and all under thirty minutes. Okay, perhaps that's a slight exaggeration (it may take closer to forty-five minutes), but frozen dessert technology has come a long way. Prices rise precipitously with each additional feature, so be prepared to pay for the luxury of a self-contained unit that can freeze simply with the flip of a switch.

For starters, let's get one thing straight: I do not recommend hand-cranked machines. They may have an irresistible nostalgic quality, and the illusion of creating a more DIY experience, but trust me here, the novelty will wear off after the first batch, if not during the first batch. These archaic machines take much longer to freeze a quart of liquid base, can be terribly messy if they require salted ice as the chilling medium, and are downright exhausting. Plan to skip your workout if you're churning ice cream by hand; the amount of labor that goes into such a process is no joke. If this hasn't yet dissuaded you, bear in mind that at the point when it becomes thicker and even harder to crank, you must actually increase your vigor to ensure that the finished ice cream has the smallest ice crystals possible, and thus smoothest, richest mouth-feel.

One of the most basic, affordable, and thus popular models is the simple freezer bowl design, which, just as the name suggests, has a separate insulated bowl that must sit in the freezer for a minimum of twenty-four hours before each batch. It's essentially a giant ice pack, shaped like a bowl, which rotates around a stationary but removable paddle. The downside is that you must plan your ice cream forays well in advance; a partially frozen bowl hastily pulled from the deep freeze will yield only slush. The big upside, however, is that $40–$50 can get you one of these babies, brand spanking new. I would argue that these modest appliances are ideal for just about everyone, from newbie ice cream creators to those with intermediate experience. This is what I employed for many years, until the base fell on the ground one time too many and cracked beyond repair. Treat your machine nicely, and it should last your whole lifetime.

If you have a stand mixer, there is likely an ice cream attachment created for your particular brand that can be purchased separately. A fine option, these are also of the freezer-bowl variety, but have the added benefit of making use of your existing appliance, saving space and hassle. Don't get me wrong, I'm a big fan of multitaskers, but there's also something to be said for specialized equipment that does one thing, and one thing very well. These types are fine options, but are actually a bit more expensive than the stand-alone sort, ringing up at about $70–$100. Additionally, when trialing the attachment designed for my KitchenAid® stand mixer, I found that the resulting ice cream was slightly icier than average.

Panicked when I had to replace my trusty freezer bowl machine, I turned to the generosity of my grandmother. It occurred to me that my grandpa had made sorbet every Thanksgiving, but since his passing, that contraption hadn't seen the light of day. Luck was on my side, because my grandma was thrilled that I would take that bulky thing off her hands, which had simply been collecting dust for nearly a decade, and also because it turned out to be a self-freezing

TROUBLESHOOTING

Ice Cream or Sorbet Too Hard?

This is, hands down, the most common complaint that I've heard (and also made myself). There are a number of culprits contributing to rock-solid, unscoopable ice cream. The key here is knowing how to manage hard ice cream, because it's not necessarily the sign of a bad recipe or a cook's error. Simply let the ice cream thaw on the counter for ten to fifteen minutes before serving, and warm your ice cream scoop or paddle in hot water before plunging into the cold, creamy depths of the container. It's helpful to let ice cream "warm" slightly regardless of the texture, as your taste buds are more capable of discerning delicate flavors when the food in question isn't eaten straight from the freezer.

Slush That Refuses to Fully Freeze?

The culprit here is an excessive measure of either sugar or alcohol, as both inhibit ice crystal formation. That's usually a good thing, but too much will prevent ice cream from solidifying at all. Your best bet is to bring the mixture back to room temperature, whisk in additional non-dairy milk to dilute the base a bit, and re-churn.

Crunchy or Icy Texture?

If you're having trouble with icy results in a particular recipe or simply want to guarantee the most luxuriously smooth texture possible, a pinch of homemade ice cream stabilizer can make a world of difference.

A generic term like "stabilizers" may sound like a euphemism for "barely food-grade chemicals of unknown origin," but fear not—there aren't any questionable additives to be found here! All of my recipes are formulated to make creamy, easily scooped frozen desserts, but to attain the level of smoothness and richness found within commercially packed pints, this little secret ingredient will do the trick. Just a tiny amount is needed, so even a small batch like the one detailed here will go a long way. Best of all, it can't go bad, so just keep the powder sealed in an airtight container and stashed in a cool place, and it can last for years if needed.

The stabilizer makes ice cream "creamier" because it inhibits ice crystals, not because it's bringing any innate creaminess to the table. You can never turn a flat-out failed custard into incredible ice cream, but it sure does help improve the texture of a frozen dessert that just needs a tiny boost in the texture department.

Homemade Ice Cream Stabilizer

2 Tablespoons Guar Gum
1 1/2 Tablespoons Xanthan Gum

1 1/2 Tablespoons Fine Soy Lecithin Powder (Not Granules)
1 Teaspoon Cornstarch

Stir everything together in an airtight container and store in a cool, dark place until needed. Using 1/4–1/2 teaspoon of the powdered blend for every quart of ice cream base, incorporate the stabilizer by constantly agitating the liquid base while slowly sprinkling in the powder. It can clump very easily, so I would suggest churning it rapidly with an immersion blender or traditional blender while adding the powdered mix.

Note: This stabilizer will not work in sorbets.

Ice Cream That's Too Sweet?

For those with a more sensitive palate and a tendency toward less sweet desserts in general, you may wish to reduce the sugar slightly in some recipes. The amount of sugar is delicately balanced, though, so it's difficult to change the amount without throwing off the carefully calibrated ratio of remaining ingredients. Alcohol is also considered a type of sugar, so you can maintain a smooth texture if the amount of alcohol is increased while the granulated or liquid sweetener is decreased. Generally, try adding 2–3 tablespoons of vodka to remove up to 1/4 cup of sugar, and don't be afraid to tweak accordingly. Bear in mind that these adjustments will inevitably alter the final flavor as well.

One of the best things about frozen desserts is that, in general, they're very forgiving. Most can be melted, tweaked, and churned all over again. Don't give up on a disappointing first spin!

BAKERY AND CANDY SHOPPE INSPIRATIONS

Baklava Ice Cream

Makes
1–1 1/2 Quarts

With a pastry so paper-thin that purists insist you can read a newspaper through it, eating baklava is one of the few situations where being "flaky" could be taken as a compliment. Though the delicate phyllo does lose some of its signature crisp texture when submerged in frozen custard for more than week or so, the walnuts hold up the fort and keep things plenty crunchy.

Toasted Cinnamon Ice Cream:

1 1/2 Teaspoons Ground Cinnamon
3 Cups Plain, Non-Dairy Milk
2 Tablespoons Cornstarch
2/3 Cup Amber Agave Nectar
1/4 Teaspoon Salt
2 Teaspoons Vanilla Extract

Walnut-Phyllo Crunch:

4 Sheets Frozen Phyllo Dough, Thawed
5 Tablespoons Non-Dairy Margarine or Coconut Oil, Melted
3/4 Cup Toasted Walnut Halves and Pieces, Chopped

3 Tablespoons Dark Brown Sugar, Firmly Packed
1/2 Teaspoon Ground Cinnamon
2 Tablespoons Amber Agave Nectar

Toasting the cinnamon brings out the full flavor of this sweet spice in addition to releasing a warm, vaguely nutty essence, and really allows it to shine. To do so, simply place the cinnamon in a small, dry skillet over low heat on the stove. Keep the skillet moving the whole time it's on the flame, just until the cinnamon becomes fragrant. Remove from the heat immediately and transfer into a small dish to prevent it from burning.

Vigorously whisk together the toasted cinnamon with the non-dairy milk and cornstarch in a medium saucepan, making sure to beat out any lumps of starch that may form. Set over moderate heat and introduce the agave and salt next. Continue whisking occasionally, scraping the bottom and sides of the pan to prevent sticking, until the mixture comes to a full boil. Immediately remove the pan from the heat, whisk in the vanilla, and let cool completely before chilling. While the base comes down to the proper temperature, you can go ahead and prepare the phyllo crunch.

Preheat your oven to 375 degrees, and line a rimmed baking sheet or jelly roll pan with parchment paper or a silpat.

Mix the melted margarine, chopped walnuts, sugar, cinnamon, and agave in a small bowl. Lay out one sheet of phyllo on your baking sheet and spread/drizzle about a third of the nut mixture on top. The whole area may not be covered, and it will certainly be lumpy and uneven, but don't worry too much about it; the whole thing will just be chopped up and mixed into your ice cream later, so it doesn't need to be gorgeous. Don't worry if you tear some of the sheets too, just keep on stacking! Cover the nuts with another sheet of phyllo, and repeat, until you've used all of the phyllo and filling.

Bake the pastry for ten to fifteen minutes, until the top is golden brown. Some of the sugar may caramelize and ooze out the sides, but as long as it doesn't burn, you needn't be too concerned. Let cool completely before chopping it into bite-sized squares. Set aside.

Once your ice cream is properly chilled, churn in your ice cream maker according to the manufacturer's instructions. While transferring the finished, soft-serve textured ice cream to an airtight container, layer scoops with your chopped phyllo and walnut pieces, covering each spoonful of soft ice cream generously. You may choose to save some of the phyllo for topping later, as it does soften over time when imbedded in the ice cream. Move the container into your freezer and let set up for at least four hours before serving.

Banana Pudding Ice Cream

Makes
Approximately
1 Quart

Often thought to be constructed only for the toothless, pudding tends to get a bad rap that it simply doesn't deserve. The milky, gelled custard that I know as pudding is like a blank canvas, waiting to be painted with all flavors and textures imaginable. One tried-and-true combination hailing from the southern U.S. states is comprised of rich vanilla pudding, crunchy vanilla cookies, and ripe, aromatic banana slices. The trio elevates the whole dessert into something much greater than the sum of its parts.

2 Tablespoons Non-Dairy Margarine, or Coconut Oil Divided
1/4 Cup Dark Brown Sugar, Firmly Packed
2 Ripe, Medium-Sized Bananas, Sliced into Quarters

1 Teaspoon Lemon Juice
2 3/4 Cups Plain, Non-Dairy Milk
2/3 Cup Granulated Sugar
2 Tablespoons Light Agave Nectar
1 Tablespoon Arrowroot
1 Tablespoon Cornstarch

Pinch Salt
1 Teaspoon Vanilla Extract
1 Cup Roughly Chopped Va'Nilla Wafer Cookies (Page 222, or Store-Bought)

Melt 1 tablespoon of the margarine or coconut oil in medium skillet or saucepan over medium-high heat until frothy. Add the brown sugar, stir well, and let bubble and cook so that the granules all dissolve; about 1 1/2 minutes. Add your chopped bananas, followed immediately by the lemon juice, and fold the fruit gently into the hot sugar so as not to break up or mash the pieces. Sauté for about two to three minutes until the bananas are softened and fragrant. Remove from the heat and chill in the fridge while focusing now on the ice cream base.

In a medium saucepan, combine the non-dairy milk, sugar, agave, arrowroot, cornstarch, and salt, whisking thoroughly so that no lumps remain. Set over medium heat and whisk occasionally until it just comes up to a full boil and has thickened significantly. Turn off the heat and stir in the remaining tablespoon of margarine or coconut oil, melting it with the residual heat. Cool to room temperature and add the vanilla. Chill thoroughly before churning in your ice cream maker according to the manufacturer's instructions.

As you transfer spoonfuls of the soft ice cream to an airtight container, fold in your sautéed bananas and sprinkle the chopped vanilla cookies over each addition as well. Give the whole thing a good mix to distribute the goodies throughout, and seal tightly before moving it to the freezer. Let solidify for at least four hours before serving.

Eat within two or three days, and you'll have delightfully crunchy cookies. Wait longer and there will be comfortingly soft pieces waiting for you that practically melt into the ice cream. Both ways are delicious.

Birthday Cake Ice Cream

Makes
1 Quart

No longer do you have to struggle with deciding between cake and ice cream; have them both in one frozen dessert! If it is simply too hot to turn on the oven, you can cheat a bit and purchase six vegan cupcakes instead of baking your own. Just scrape off the frosting before blending them up.

Vanilla Cupcakes:

1/2 Cup Plain, Non-Dairy Milk
1/2 Teaspoon Apple Cider Vinegar
1 1/2 Teaspoons Vanilla Extract
3 Tablespoons Canola Oil

3/4 Cup All-Purpose Flour, or All-Purpose Gluten-Free Flour Blend
1/3 Cup Granulated Sugar
1/2 Teaspoon Baking Powder
1/4 Teaspoon Baking Soda
Pinch Salt

Ice Cream Base:

1 1/2 Cups Plain Non-Dairy Milk
1/2 Cup Granulated Sugar
2–4 Tablespoons Sprinkles (Page 212 or Store-Bought)

Preheat your oven to 350 degrees, and lightly grease six muffin tins.* Set aside.

Combine the non-dairy milk, vinegar, vanilla, and oil in a small bowl, whisk thoroughly, and let sit for five minutes.

In a separate bowl, sift together the flour, sugar, baking powder, baking soda, and salt. Whisk to distribute all of the dry goods evenly; then pour the wet ingredients into the bowl of dry. Stir just enough to bring the batter together; a few errant lumps are fine.

Distribute the batter equally between your prepared muffin tins, and bake for eighteen to twenty-two minutes until golden brown and a toothpick inserted into the center comes out clean. Let cool completely before proceeding.

For a fun twist, instead of moving the finished ice cream into a container to be served up in scoops, pack the soft ice cream into sturdy cupcake cups and let freeze solid. Right before eating or presenting them, pipe or spoon a dollop of frosting on top. Voilà, a genuine ice cream cupcake!

Toss the cooled cupcakes into your food processor or blender, along with the soymilk and sugar to make the ice cream base. Purée thoroughly, until completely smooth. Chill for at least one hour in the refrigerator before churning in your ice cream maker according to the manufacturer's instructions. In the last five minutes of churning, add in your sprinkles.

Transfer the soft ice cream into an airtight container and let rest in the freezer for at least three hours before serving, until solid enough to scoop.

*Don't touch those cupcake papers! Not only would it be wasteful since they would immediately be discarded, but giving the batter more contact with the pan ensures better browning, which means more caramelization, which ultimately means more flavor!

Blue Moon Ice Cream

Makes About
1 Quart

Amysterious flavor with a storied history, the actual taste and composition of blue moon ice cream is rather controversial. Some say that it tastes like bubble gum; others, marshmallows. As for me, I remember it being more like a certain fruity cereal I used to favor. The only thing that everyone can agree on is that the color absolutely must be an other-wordly vibrant shade of blue. It's a bright and playful option that children tend to adore, and adults are not soon to forget. This is also a great opportunity to get the kids into the kitchen—have them help you by picking out all the blue cereal loops!

3 Cups Plain, Non-Dairy Milk

2 Cups Fruit Ring Cereal, Blue Pieces Only

2/3 Cup Granulated Sugar

2 Tablespoons Arrowroot

1/4 Teaspoon Salt

1/2 Teaspoon Vanilla Extract

Set a medium saucepan over moderate heat and stir in the non-dairy milk and cereal to combine. Bring the mixture up to a boil, cover, and turn off the heat. Let the "milk" infuse for about an hour; the cereal pieces will be very soft, and the liquid will have turned blue. Transfer everything into a blender, and thoroughly purée. Pass the blended mix through a strainer and discard any solids.

Return the blue liquid to the same saucepan, and vigorously whisk in the sugar, arrowroot, and salt, double-checking that no lumps remain before turning on the burner to medium heat. Whisk occasionally until it comes to a full boil, and let bubble away for one minute longer. Remove from the heat, whisk in the vanilla, and let cool to room temperature before transferring to the fridge to cool completely. Give it at least three hours to chill through and through.

Churn in your ice cream machine according to the manufacturer's directions. Transfer the soft ice cream to an air-tight container, and store it in the freezer for another three hours minimum, until frozen solid, before serving.

Brown Sugar-Licorice Ice Cream

Makes About
1 Quart

Apolarizing ingredient to say the least, licorice is best used with caution. Either you love it or you hate it. Brown sugar complements the dark, tannic flavor of licorice, which is found in the form of chewy candies sprinkled throughout for a delightful surprise in every bite. Though the base could work just as well with any nut, chocolate chip, or cookie mix-in, give licorice a fair chance to redeem itself; ice cream can improve anything, if you ask me!

3 Cups Plain, Non-Dairy Milk
1 Cup Dark Brown Sugar, Firmly
 Packed
2 Tablespoons Cornstarch

1 Tablespoon Arrowroot
1/2 Teaspoon Salt
3/4 Teaspoon Vanilla Extract
1/4 Teaspoon Almond Extract

2/3 Cup Chopped Black Licorice
 Candy

In a medium saucepan, combine the non-dairy milk, brown sugar, cornstarch, arrowroot, and salt. Before turning on the heat, beat thoroughly to break up all lumps, big and small. Turn the flame up to medium and whisk occasionally, until the mixture comes to a boil. Let cook at a full boil for two additional minutes; then remove the pan from the burner. Add in the vanilla and almond extract, stirring to incorporate.

Let cool to room temperature and then chill thoroughly for at least three hours before churning in your ice cream machine according to the manufacturer's directions. In the last five minutes of churning, slowly sprinkle in the chopped licorice candy so that the moving paddle of the machine incorporates and distributes the pieces throughout the ice cream. Transfer the soft ice cream to an airtight container, and store it in the freezer for another three hours minimum, or until frozen solid, before serving.

Buttery Popcorn Ice Cream

Makes About
1 Quart

An addictive snack to begin with, a handful of salty, buttery popcorn is hard to refuse. It might not sound like a flavor that translates well into an ice cream recipe, but this is one that you've got to try for yourself. A little bit savory and sweet at the same time, with a slightly caramel-like flavor thanks to the brown sugar, this is one delight that you definitely won't find at your average carnival.

1/2 Cup Unpopped Popcorn Kernels
2 1/2 Cups Plain, Non-Dairy Milk
1/3 Cup Granulated Sugar

1/3 Cup Dark Brown Sugar, Firmly
    Packed
1/2 Teaspoon Nutritional Yeast

1/2 Teaspoon Salt
1/2 Cup Non-Dairy Margarine,
    Melted

Place the popcorn kernels in a medium-sized brown paper bag (if you're not sure if it's big enough, err on the side of caution and pop the corn in two separate batches). Use transparent or masking tape to seal the bag shut, and put it in the microwave. Use the "popcorn" setting if possible, or set the timer for 3 1/2 minutes at full power. When the popping slows to about once every five seconds, remove the bag and open it very carefully, making sure your hands and face are out of the way—the steam can be quite painful! Sift out all of the unpopped kernels.

Move the popped corn into your food processor or blender, and add in the non-dairy milk, both sugars, nutritional yeast, and salt. Thoroughly purée for two to three minutes, until smooth. With the motor running, very slowly drizzle in the melted margarine, as if making a salad dressing, to create an emulsification. Pass the mixture through a fine strainer to ensure a silky smooth texture, if desired.

Chill for at least one hour in the refrigerator before churning in your ice cream maker according to the manufacturer's instructions.

Transfer the soft ice cream into an airtight container and let rest in the freezer for at least three hours before serving, until solid enough to scoop.

> Fond of that old ballpark classic, Cracker Jack? Replicate that crunchy snack in a creamier format with just a few alterations! Make this ice cream with all brown sugar, and throw in ½ cup of roughly chopped peanuts in the last five minutes of churning for a similar taste sensation.

Cheesecake Ice Cream

Makes About
1 Quart

Talk about instant gratification: You can go from ingredients to ice cream in under an hour with this fool-proof and highly versatile formula! Tasting for all the world like the filling of a frozen cheesecake, no baking or fussing necessary, it's the kind of frozen treat you can serve at the end of a fancy meal or for a quiet evening at home.

For crust lovers, go ahead and pile it on as thick as you like with a sprinkling of crushed graham crackers (page 203) over each serving.

1 8-Ounce Container Vegan "Cream Cheese"
1/4 Cup Vegan "Sour Cream"
3/4 Cup Light Agave Nectar

1 Tablespoon Vanilla Extract
2 Cups Plain, Non-Dairy Milk
Pinch Salt

3/4 Cup Jam of Choice (Blueberry, Strawberry, Cherry, etc. Try combining flavors, too!)

A recipe this simple hardly even needs to be written out, but here goes. Pile everything but the jam into your blender and purée briefly, just until smooth. Blend no longer than necessary, to prevent the mixture from warming up.

Pour the ice cream base into your ice cream maker and churn according to the manufacturer's instructions. Spoon the soft ice cream into an airtight container, and in between spoonfuls, dollop your desired flavor of jam. Swirl the whole mixture together lightly so that there's a colorful ripple of jam all throughout. Chill the ice cream in the freezer for at least three hours before serving, until solid enough to scoop.

Cinnamon-Graham Ice Cream

Makes About
1 Quart

Sweets-seeking missiles, pillaging the cupboards of our unsuspecting grandparents' kitchens on every visit, my sister and I were two sugar fiends on a mission in our heyday. Wise to our tactic, it was my Nana who instituted the "cookie jar" early on, stocked with wholesome graham crackers. The cinnamon-sugar dusted variety was my first choice and can still stir up homey, comforting feelings today.

2 1/2 Cups Plain, Non-Dairy Milk
1/2 Cup Full-Fat Coconut Milk
5 Rectangle Sheets or 10 Squares
     Graham Crackers, Crushed

2/3 Cup Granulated Sugar
2 Tablespoons Cornstarch
1 Teaspoon Ground Cinnamon
1 Teaspoon Vanilla Extract

3 Rectangle Sheets or 6 Squares
     Graham Crackers, Roughly
     Broken Into Bite-Sized Pieces

Place the non-dairy milk, coconut milk, crushed graham crackers, sugar, cornstarch, and cinnamon in your blender and purée until completely smooth. Pass the mixture through a strainer to remove any sediment and discard the solids. Transfer to a medium saucepan and set over moderate heat.

Bring to a boil, whisking occasionally, until the liquid comes to a rolling boil and has thickened in consistency. Turn off the heat immediately, whisk in the vanilla, and let cool to room temperature before chilling in the fridge for at least three hours before churning.

Process in your ice cream maker according to the manufacturer's instructions, adding in the remaining graham cracker pieces in the last five minutes of churning. Transfer to an airtight container and freeze solidly for at least three hours before serving.

Cookie Monster Ice Cream

Makes About
1 1/2 Quarts

Regular cookie dough ice cream is on the path to greatness, but just doesn't go quite far enough for the true cookie monster at heart. For one thing, the prized mix-ins are never plentiful enough, and spoonful after spoonful of plain vanilla ice cream becomes painfully monotonous. It only needs the addition of a few chopped sandwich cookies to elevate this promising offering into something even better. Like a mash-up of cookies 'n' crème and cookie dough, this ice cream is positively loaded with goodies in every single bite. Even your usual accompaniment of non-dairy milk is included here!

Ice Cream Base:

3 Cups Plain, Non-Dairy Milk
3 Tablespoons Cornstarch
2/3 Cup Granulated Sugar
1/4 Teaspoon Salt
2 Teaspoons Vanilla Extract

Chocolate Chip Cookie Dough:

1 Tablespoon Non-Dairy Margarine
1/4 Cup Granulated Sugar
1/4 Cup Dark Brown Sugar, Firmly
   Packed
1/2 Cup All-Purpose Flour
1/8 Teaspoon Salt

2 Tablespoons Mini Semi-Sweet
   Chocolate Chips, or Finely
   Chopped Semi-Sweet Chocolate
1/4 Teaspoon Vanilla Extract
1–2 Tablespoons Plain, Non-Dairy
   Milk
1 Cup Quartered Chocolate
   Crème-Filled Sandwich Cookies
   (About 10)

In a medium saucepan, combine the non-dairy milk, cornstarch, sugar, and salt. Whisk vigorously before turning on the heat. Turn the burner up to medium heat and whisk occasionally, until the mixture comes up to a boil. Let cook at a full boil for two additional minutes, and then remove the pan from the heat. Add in the vanilla, stirring to incorporate. Let cool to room temperature and then chill thoroughly for at least three hours.

Meanwhile, prepare the cookie dough. Melt the margarine, and combine it with both sugars, flour, salt, and chocolate chips. Stir in the vanilla; then drizzle the non-dairy milk in slowly, one tablespoon at a time, until the mixture comes together into a cohesive dough. Mix well so that no pockets of dry ingredients remain (you may choose to use a stand mixer if you have one, but it's not strictly necessary). Scoop the dough into small balls, varying somewhere between the size of raisins and walnuts, placing them on an aluminum foil-lined baking sheet. Stash the sheet in your freezer so that the balls can firm up a bit.

Once properly chilled, churn the ice cream base in your ice cream machine according to the manufacturer's directions. Transfer spoonfuls of the soft ice cream into an airtight container, sprinkling quartered sandwich cookies and balls of frozen cookie dough over each addition. Fold the last addition in with a wide spatula, scooping all the way to the bottom and out, to fully mix and distribute all of the cookie add-ins. Stash the ice cream in your freezer for at least three hours before serving.

Easy as Pumpkin Pie Ice Cream

Makes About
1 Quart

It's just not Thanksgiving without pumpkin pie. Even more critical than the mashed potatoes or the grand roast (be it tofu or otherwise), a harvest feast is woefully incomplete without that spicy pumpkin custard on the table. The trouble is, after such a huge banquet it can be a stretch, quite literally, to fit in a full slice of pie. Without the crust or size constraints, a lighter, refreshing scoop of pumpkin pie ice cream is definitely the way to go.

1 Cup Solid-Pack Pumpkin Purée
1 14-Ounce Can (1 ¾ Cup) Full-Fat
   Coconut Milk
1/2 Cup Dark Brown Sugar, Packed

1/4 Cup Grade-B Maple Syrup
2 Tablespoons Bourbon or Dark Rum
1 1/2 Teaspoons Ground Cinnamon
3/4 Teaspoon Ground Ginger

1/4 Teaspoon Ground Cloves
Pinch Freshly Cracked Black Pepper
1/4 Teaspoon Salt
1 Teaspoon Vanilla Extract

As the title implies, this recipe could hardly be any easier. Just take all of the ingredients and mix them together in a big bowl until smooth and homogeneous. Chill if not already cold, and process in your ice cream machine as per the manufacturer's instructions. Transfer into an airtight container and freeze until solid before serving; at least three hours. Serve with whipped crème, spiffy whip (page 216), butterscotch sauce (page 196), or simply a long nap afterwards!

French Toast Ice Cream

Makes
1–1 1/2 Quarts

Bread that goes stale quickly should be seen as a sign of quality. Only lesser loaves, pumped full of preservatives, would last for weeks on the counter. Real bread has a surprisingly short shelf-life, which means there are inevitably many stale ends to contend with for anyone that buys it regularly. The usual French toast approach gets old after a few consecutive breakfasts, but that's no reason to scrap the whole concept. Rather, try churning up a creamy, frozen version!

6 Ounces Stale Bread*
2 1/2 Cups Plain, Non-Dairy Milk, Divided
1/2 Cup Grade-B Maple Syrup

1/3 Cup Dark Brown Sugar, Firmly Packed
1 1/2 Teaspoons Ground Cinnamon
1 Tablespoon Nutritional Yeast
Pinch Salt

Pinch Nutmeg
1/4 Cup Non-Dairy Margarine, Melted

Lightly toast each slice of bread to a golden-brown color before tearing or chopping into small pieces. Place in a large bowl, and set aside.

Whisk together the non-dairy milk, maple syrup, brown sugar, cinnamon, nutritional yeast, salt, and nutmeg. Pour this liquid mixture over the bread, making sure all the pieces are covered. Let soak for about thirty minutes so that the bread can soften and begin to absorb the "milk."

Transfer all of the soaked bread and the remaining liquid to your blender, and thoroughly purée. While the motor is running, slowly stream in the melted margarine to form an emulsion, much the same way you would if making salad dressing. Once fully incorporated and smooth, pass the base through a fine mesh strainer and chill thoroughly before churning.

Churn in your ice cream maker according to the manufacturer's instructions. Store the ice cream in an airtight container, and let set up in the freezer for at least three hours before serving.

*For sandwich bread, one slice usually weighs in right around 1 ounce, but varies depending on the loaf. Most varieties will work fine here, so feel free to just make use of what's on hand, but white bread makes for the most dessert-like treat.

Oatmeal Raisin Ice Cream

Makes About
1 Quart

Considering the popularity of chocolate chip cookie dough ice cream, I'm surprised there aren't more cookie-centric frozen desserts. Some just seem like a natural fit, such as the oatmeal cookie. Hearty, homey, and simply comforting, I couldn't resist the temptation. Although there are no actual pieces of cookies or raw dough included, each spoonful tastes like a creamy, chilly mouthful of pure oatmeal cookie heaven.

Oatmeal Raisin Ice Cream:

2 2/3 Cups Plain, Non-Dairy Milk
1/2 Cup Old-Fashioned Rolled Oats, Finely Ground
1/2 Teaspoon Salt
1 1/2 Teaspoons Ground Cinnamon
2/3 Cup Dark Brown Sugar, Firmly Packed
1/2 Cup Raisins*
3 Tablespoons Margarine or Coconut Oil, Melted
1 Teaspoon Vanilla Extract

Oatmeal Praline:

1/3 Cup Old-Fashioned Rolled Oats
1/4 Cup Granulated Sugar
1 Tablespoon Light Corn Syrup or Agave Nectar
1 Tablespoon Water
Pinch Salt

In a medium saucepan, whisk together the non-dairy milk, oat flour, salt, cinnamon, brown sugar, and raisins, making sure that there are no errant lumps of flour remaining before turning on the heat. Although it may seem awkward to cook the custard with the raisins, it's important to include them from the start so that they rehydrate a bit, which will prevent them from freezing into solid little rocks in the final ice cream.

Set over medium heat and whisk gently until the liquid is significantly thickened and bubbles begin to break on the surface. Remove from the heat, and while whisking vigorously, slowly drizzle in the melted margarine or coconut oil in a thin stream. Finally, stir in the vanilla, and let cool. Chill thoroughly in the refrigerator for at least one hour.

Meanwhile, you can make the oatmeal praline. Place the rolled oats in a dry skillet, and toast them over medium heat, stirring all the while. After five to eight minutes, the oats should be golden brown and fragrant, at which time you should move them to a medium bowl to cool.

Prepare for the final praline by laying out a silpat or lightly greased baking sheet. In a separate microwave-safe bowl, combine the sugar, syrup or agave, water, and salt. Microwave the mixture for about 1 1/2 minutes; then stir thoroughly. Return it to the microwave for an additional one to two minutes, until boiling and bubbling vigorously; then quickly pour it over the oats. Stir to incorporate; then pour the sugared oats onto your prepared silpat. Use your spatula to smooth it out into as thin a layer as possible. Let cool and harden completely. Break into bite-sized pieces.

Churn the ice cream base in your ice cream maker according to the manufacturer's instructions, and in the last five minutes of churning, sprinkle in the pieces of oatmeal praline.

Transfer the soft ice cream into an airtight container, and let rest in the freezer for at least three hours before serving, until solid enough to scoop.

*Sun-dried grapes with a concentrated burst of sweetness, raisins are a delightful little snack if you ask me, but they can be a surprisingly polarizing ingredient when it comes to dessert. For all of those raisin-haters out there, go ahead and substitute chocolate chips instead. I may disagree with the preference, but I wouldn't complain about a chocolate variation. Just throw them into the machine in the final five minutes of churning, rather than cooking them into the custard.

Peppermint Crush Ice Cream

Makes About
1 Quart

As I stalked the freezer cases of my local grocery store, there was one thing that announced the arrival of the holiday season when I was younger—peppermint stick ice cream. That elusive flavor was the highlight of those dark, dreary December days, and would always be so difficult to bid farewell to as spring approached. Happily, the homemade version doesn't have to be a "limited edition," and it has higher quality ingredients that better suit a more grown-up palate.

25 Starlight Peppermint Hard
    Candies*
2 Cups Plain, Non-Dairy milk

3/4 Cup Full-Fat Coconut Milk
2/3 Cup Granulated Sugar
2 Tablespoons Arrowroot Powder

1 Teaspoon Vanilla Extract
3 Tablespoons Crème De Menthe

Begin by unwrapping all of the mint candies and placing them in your blender or food processor. Pulse repeatedly until the candies become a coarse meal, looking much like tiny pebbles surrounded by a bit of sand. Warning: This will be very loud at first! Set aside.

In a medium saucepan, combine the non-dairy milk, coconut milk, sugar, and arrowroot powder. Whisk thoroughly to ensure that there are no clumps of arrowroot remaining in the liquid before placing the pan on the stove over medium heat. Whisk occasionally until the liquid comes right up to the brink of boiling, with bubbles breaking actively on the surface. Remove from the heat and stir in the vanilla and crème de menthe. Let cool for a few minutes before transferring the base to the refrigerator, where it should chill thoroughly before proceeding.

Churn in your ice cream maker according to the manufacturer's instructions.

Transfer the soft ice cream into an airtight container; intersperse each scoop of fresh ice cream with a sprinkling of the ground-up mint candies, creating layers of ice cream and peppermints. Let rest in the freezer for at least three hours before serving, until solid enough to scoop.

*Starlight candies are easier to find year-round, but you can use eight regular size candy canes instead if you have them on hand.

Pfeffernüsse Ice Cream

**Makes About
1 Quart**

Imagine gingerbread, but with an emphasis on anise rather than ginger, and you'd come pretty close to the spicy flavor of pfeffernüsse. A German cookie which translates roughly to "pepper nuts," they're a classic treat for the holidays, but it's hard to resist their allure even in the heat of summer. Rather than slaving over a hot oven, churn up a chillier rendition. Slightly sharper than your average gingersnap, it's still demure enough for those with timid palates to enjoy.

3 Cups Plain, Non-Dairy Milk
3/4 Cup Granulated Sugar
2 Tablespoons Molasses
1 1/2 Tablespoons Arrowroot Powder
1 Tablespoon All-Purpose Flour or All-
    Purpose Gluten-Free Flour Blend

2 Teaspoons Ground Star Anise,
    Anise Seed, or Fennel Seed
1 1/2 Teaspoon Ground Cinnamon
1/2 Teaspoon Ground Cloves
1/4 Teaspoon Ground Cardamom
1/4 Teaspoon Ground White Pepper

1/4 Teaspoon Salt
1 Tablespoon Non-Dairy Margarine
1/2 Teaspoon Almond Extract

In a medium saucepan, vigorously whisk together the non-dairy milk, sugar, molasses, arrowroot, flour, all of the spices, and salt. Make sure that there are no lumps remaining before turning on the heat to medium. Whisk occasionally until it just comes up to a rolling boil and has thickened significantly. Remove from the heat and toss in the margarine, using the residual heat to melt it into the mixture. Cool completely and finally whisk in the almond extract.

Chill thoroughly before churning in your ice cream maker according to the manufacturer's instructions. Transfer to an airtight container, and freeze solidly for at least three hours before serving.

Red Hot Ice Cream

Makes About
1 Quart

"Hot pink" is more like it as far as color is concerned. However, this flamboyantly colored ice cream actually has a pretty fierce bite! Hot ice cream may sound like a hoax, but thanks to a generous measure of Red Hot candies, the spicier side of cinnamon blazes brightly through the sub-freezing serving temperature.

3 Cups Plain, Non-Dairy Milk
1/4 Cup Granulated Sugar

1 1/2 Tablespoons Arrowroot
1 Cup Red Hot Candies,* Divided

1 Teaspoon Vanilla Extract

Vigorously whisk together the non-dairy milk, sugar, and arrowroot in a medium saucepan, beating thoroughly to break up any possible clumps of starch. Set over moderate heat and add in ¾ cup of the red hot candies, setting ¼ cup aside for later.

The candies will slowly melt into the liquid, turning it deeper and deeper red. It only turns pink during the freezing process, since the air that gets folded in as it churns lightens the mixture.

Bring to a boil, whisking occasionally, at which point the liquid should be considerably thickened with no solid pieces of candy remaining. Turn off the heat and whisk in the vanilla. Cool to room temperature before chilling for at least three hours before proceeding.

Churn in your ice cream maker according to the manufacturer's instructions. Scoop dollops of the soft ice cream into an airtight container and sprinkle a handful of the remaining Red Hots over each addition. Mix the whole thing thoroughly with a wide spatula to evenly distribute all of the candy pieces, and let set up in the freezer for at least three hours before serving.

*Also known as *Cinnamon Imperials*, not all brands of Red Hots are vegan thanks to a coating of beeswax. Read labels scrupulously and be on the lookout for those made by Brach's® and Ferrara Pan Candy Company® specifically, which are "accidentally" vegan.

Red Velvet Ice Cream

Makes About
1 Quart

A truly sweet southern belle if I ever did know one, red velvet cake is perhaps one of the most instantly recognizable, albeit controversial, classic American desserts. Said to have begun as a consequence of natural cocoa powder reacting to an acidic environment in the batter, thus turning red when baked, most attempts nowadays involve at least a full bottle of artificial food coloring to carry the hue.

For a more natural red velvet, I prefer to employ red beets for the task. Some may even consider this a more "authentic" route, as it's rumored that bakers resorted to incorporating this brilliant root vegetable into their cakes during World War II, when other luxuries were harder to come by. Though it may contribute a very slight earthy flavor, it's a far better solution than a bitter brew of colored chemicals.

Red Velvet Ice Cream Base:

3 Tablespoons Cornstarch
3 Tablespoons Natural Cocoa Powder
3/4 Cup Granulated Sugar
Pinch Salt
2 Cups Plain Vegan Creamer

2/3 Cup Beet Juice
1/3 Cup Full-Fat Coconut Milk
1 1/2 Teaspoons Vanilla Extract
1/2 Teaspoon White Vinegar

"Cream Cheese" Frosting Swirl:

4 Ounces (1/2 Package) Vegan "Cream Cheese"
1/4 Cup Light Agave Nectar or Corn Syrup
1/2 Teaspoon Vanilla Extract

In a medium saucepan, whisk together the cornstarch, cocoa, sugar, and salt, distributing the cocoa and starch evenly throughout the mixture to prevent lumps from forming later. In a separate bowl, combine the creamer, beet juice, and coconut milk before pouring a splash (about 1/2 cup) into the saucepan. Whisk it into a thick paste, incorporating all of the dry goods and stirring until smooth, before pouring in the remainder of the liquid.

Turn on the heat to medium, and continue whisking occasionally. Cook until it reaches a rolling boil and is thickened significantly; then turn off the heat. Add in the vanilla and vinegar, and whisk vigorously to incorporate. Let cool completely before stashing in your fridge to chill for at least three hours before churning.

Churn in your ice cream maker according to the manufacturer's instructions. Meanwhile, mix together all of the ingredients for the "cream cheese" swirl, until smooth. Once the ice cream is ready, scoop dollops out of the machine and into an airtight container, drizzling a generous amount of the "cream cheese" mixture over each addition. Use a wide spatula to lightly marble the whole container of ice cream; then quickly move it into the freezer to solidify. Let freeze for at least three hours before serving.

Sesame Halvah Ice Cream

Makes 1 Loaf or 2
Mini Loaves; About
8–10 Servings

Dense, chewy, very rich, and often tooth-achingly sweet, halvah is a candy reserved for special occasions and meant for sharing. Scores of flavor variations exist, but the top sellers are unarguably any sort with chocolate (especially those with a hypnotizing cocoa swirl marbled throughout) and pistachios. Serving this frozen rendition in loaf format is completely optional, but since it's no additional effort and such a whimsical presentation, why not go all out and play a bit with your food?

Sesame Ice Cream Base:

1 Cup Tahini*
3/4 Cup Granulated Sugar
1 1/2 Tablespoons Cornstarch
1/2 Teaspoon Salt
2/3 Cup Plain, Non-Dairy Milk

1 1/3 Cups Full-Fat Coconut Milk
1 1/2 Teaspoons Vanilla Extract

Pistachio Halvah Option:

1/2 Cup Shelled and Roasted
(Unsalted) Pistachios

OR

Chocolate Halvah Option:

2 Ounces (1/3 Cup) Semi-Sweet
Chocolate Chips
1 Teaspoon Olive Oil

In a medium saucepan, vigorously whisk together the tahini, sugar, cornstarch, and salt, to help break up the sticky seed butter. While actively whisking the mixture, drizzle in the non-dairy milk and coconut milk until fully incorporated and homogeneous. Make sure that there are no lumps remaining, and place on the stove over medium heat. Whisk gently while the base cooks, until bubbles begin to break on the surface and the liquid is significantly thickened. Remove from the heat and stir in the vanilla. Let cool before moving the mixture into the fridge. Chill for at least three hours before churning in your ice cream machine according to the manufacturer's instructions.

Line a 4 x 8-inch loaf pan with aluminum foil, and lightly grease. Set aside.

For the pistachio halvah option, add the pistachios into the machine within the last five minutes of churning.

For the chocolate option, melt together the chocolate and oil by heating on high at thirty-second intervals in the microwave, stirring thoroughly between each heating, until smooth. When the ice cream is done churning, scoop it out

> Can't make up your mind about which flavor variation to choose? Go for both! Use half of the amounts called for, and split up the base between two foil-lined and lightly greased 3 x 5-inch mini loaf pans.

into a large bowl, and drizzle the melted chocolate in a thin stream. Quickly fold the chocolate ribbon in with a wide spatula, being careful to marble it but not fully incorporate it.

Scoop the soft ice cream into your prepared loaf pan, cover tightly with plastic wrap, and stash in the freezer for at least four to six hours to fully solidify. To serve, flip the whole loaf out onto a plate, peel away the foil, and slice as desired.

*Tahini has a tendency to separate more severely than other nut or seed butters, so before each usage, stir up the whole jar vigorously, from top to bottom.

Sour Cherry Pie Ice Cream

**Makes
1 1/2 Quarts**

Cherry season is like Christmas: greatly anticipated throughout the year, far too short, and full of sweet gratification. After gorging and often overdosing on sweet cherries, the astringent pucker-power of sour cherries is a welcome change of pace. Rarely given the respect they deserve, sour cherries are often cooked to death and drowned in sugar to make up for their lack of sweetness. Such a shameful waste: their uniquely tart flavor should be celebrated rather than covered up!

Sour Cherry Ice Cream:

2 Cups Whole Sour Cherries, Pits
    and Stems Removed (About
    13–14 Ounces Pitted)
1/2 Cup Granulated Sugar
1 Tablespoon Lemon Juice
1/4 Teaspoon Salt

1 1/2 Cups Plain, Non-Dairy Milk
1 Tablespoon Cornstarch
1/4 Teaspoon Almond Extract

Pie Crust Streusel:

1/2 Cup All-Purpose Flour or All-
    Purpose Gluten-Free Flour Blend
    (Page vi)

1 Teaspoon Granulated Sugar
Pinch Salt
3 Tablespoons Non-Dairy Margarine
1–2 Tablespoons Ice Cold Water

First, begin with the sour cherry ice cream base. In a medium saucepan, cook the cherries, sugar, lemon juice, and salt over medium heat, bringing the mixture up to a steady but gentle bubble. Turn down the heat slightly so that the cherries continue to stew at the same rate for about twenty to twenty-five minutes, until the fruits are almost entirely broken down and the remaining liquid is very thick and syrupy. Roughly mash the cherries with your spatula or a potato masher.

Whisk together the non-dairy milk and cornstarch in a separate container, breaking up any lumps of starch that may form, before adding both into the saucepan. Continue to stir until the mixture comes back up to a boil. Cook for a minute longer, remove from the heat, and finally add in the almond extract. Let cool before chilling in your fridge for at least three hours.

Meanwhile, prepare the crust streusel. Preheat your oven to 350 degrees, and line a baking sheet with parchment paper or a silpat. Combine the flour, sugar, and salt in a large bowl, and cut the margarine into small pieces before tossing them in as well. Use a pastry cutter or two forks to continue cutting in the margarine, until you achieve a coarse, meal-like consistency. Drizzle in the water, 1 teaspoon at

> Sour cherries can be tough to track down, so if dark, sweet cherries are the only options in town, you can still make a very delicious ice cream. It won't be exactly the same, but simply increase the lemon juice to three tablespoons for a similarly sour bite.

a time, just until you can mix together the ingredients to form a cohesive dough. Be careful not to overwork the dough, as that will create a tough crust.

Using a lightly floured rolling pin, roll out your dough on the prepared baking sheet to about 1/8–1/4-inch thickness. Roughly tear or chop the crust into bite-sized pieces and spread them apart on the sheet so that there's more room for the hot air to circulate. Bake for ten to fifteen minutes, until golden brown around the edges. Let cool completely; then stash in the freezer so that they're as cold as possible when it comes time for them to meet the ice cream. You should have about 3/4–1 cup of crust pieces.

Churn the ice cream in your machine according to manufacturer's instructions. Transfer scoops of the soft ice cream into an airtight container, and top each addition with a layer of pie crust streusel. Repeat until both ice cream and crust are used up. Let the ice cream set up in the freezer for at least three hours before scooping and serving.

Tiramisu Ice Cream

Makes
1–1 1/2 Quarts

Tiramisu and I are no strangers, though most encounters are not in its usual coffee-infused format. I've enjoyed a Japanese-fusion matcha tiramisu, as well as a mimosa rendition. Returning to the more widely accepted notion of lady fingers, mascarpone, and coffee, tiramisu ice cream delivers a sweet pick-me-up without the fuss of assembly. Vegan "sour cream" lends that cheesy twang that mascarpone would bring to the party, and homemade lady fingers go the extra mile to create something special. After trying the traditional set of flavors and components, I can see why it's an enduring classical dessert.

"Mascarpone" Ice Cream:

2 Cups Plain, Non-Dairy Milk
1 Tablespoon Arrowroot
1 Cup Vegan "Sour Cream"
2/3 Cup Granulated Sugar
1 Teaspoon Vanilla Extract
Tiny Pinch Lemon Zest

1 Tablespoon Kahlua or Coffee
    Liqueur

Lady Fingers:

1/4 Cup Granulated Sugar
1 Teaspoon Cornstarch
1/2 Cup Cake Flour
1/2 Teaspoon Baking Powder

1/4 Cup Plain Soy or Coconut Yogurt
1/4 Teaspoon Apple Cider Vinegar
1/4 Teaspoon Vanilla Extract
Confectioner's Sugar, As Needed

For Assembly:

1/4 Cup Kahlua or Coffee Liqueur
1 Teaspoon Instant Coffee Powder

In a medium saucepan, first whisk together the non-dairy milk and arrowroot vigorously, taking care to beat out any possible lumps of starch. Add in the "sour cream" and sugar, whisking until smooth. Turn on the heat to medium, and stir occasionally, until the mixture comes up to a full boil. Immediately remove the pan from the heat and stir in the vanilla, lemon zest, and kahlua. Cool before thoroughly chilling in the fridge, at least three hours, before churning.

To make the lady fingers, preheat your oven to 350 degrees and line two baking sheets with silpats.

In a medium bowl, sift together the sugar, cornstarch, flour, and baking powder, mixing to evenly distribute all of the dry ingredients.

Another unforgettable Italian dessert, the cannoli, is also just as easy to emulate with this ice cream base: Omit the lady fingers, Kahlua, and instant coffee, but mix 1 tablespoon of Grand Marnier or limoncello into the base instead. Once churned, fold in approximately 3/4–1 cup of broken ice cream cone pieces to mimic the cannoli shell, along with 1/3 cup of either mini chocolate chips or chopped pistachios.

In a separate bowl, mix together the yogurt, vinegar, and vanilla. Pour the yogurt mixture into the dry goods, and mix with a wide spatula. It will seem very dry at first, but trust me, you won't need any more liquid; just keep stirring until it comes together into a thick, rather stiff batter. Spoon the batter into a piping bag fitted with a large, round tip (about 1/2 inch) and pipe 3-inch-long strips onto your prepared sheets, spacing each about 1 inch apart.

Sprinkle a light coat of confectioner's sugar over the cookies with a sifter or fine mesh strainer, and bake for nine to twelve minutes, until the cookies no longer appear shiny and are just barely browned around the edges. You should end up with about one dozen lady fingers.

Once cool, proceed to churn the "mascarpone" ice cream in your machine according to the manufacturer's instructions. Meanwhile, mix together the remaining kahlua and coffee powder until the granules are dissolved, and have your airtight storage container ready. Work as quickly as possible to prevent melting, and scoop out a layer of freshly churned ice cream into the bottom of the container. Dip lady fingers in the kahlua and instant coffee mixture so that they can soak some of it in, but not so much that they dissolve. Press half of the lady fingers into the layer of ice cream, and top with a second layer of soft ice cream. Repeat with the remaining lady fingers, and finish by smoothing any leftover ice cream over the top. Seal the container and stash in your freezer for at least four hours before serving. You can either serve scoops like you would for any other flavor, or cut wedges as if it were a whole frozen tiramisu.

Toasted Marshmallow Ice Cream

Makes
1 Scant Quart

Any girl scout or boy scout worth their badges can tell you that the best part of camping is gathering around a roaring fire, sticking fluffy little marshmallows on pointed twigs, and incinerating them to a blacker shade of burnt. Hopefully most of us move beyond that stage and learn to appreciate the more carefully tended, golden, and ash-free version. This basic ice cream recipe is practically begging to be made into frozen s'mores, but I happen to think it makes an incredible base for vanilla bean milkshakes, too.

1 10-Ounce Container Ricemellow
 Crème, or 10 Ounces Vegan
 Marshmallows

2 Cups Plain, Non-Dairy Milk
2 Teaspoons Vanilla Extract
Pinch Salt

Heat the broiler of your oven to high and generously grease a jelly roll pan or rimmed baking sheet. Spread the mallow crème out in a thin, even layer or sprinkle on the marshmallows so that none overlap. Broil for five to ten minutes, until the top is golden brown and bubbly, and your kitchen smells like a sweet campfire. Keep a very close eye on the oven the whole time, because as any camper can tell you, marshmallows go from perfectly toasted and delicious to positively incinerated in no time. Cool for fifteen to thirty minutes before proceeding.

Scrape the toasted marshmallow crème or plain marshmallows off the baking sheet and into your blender. Add in the remaining ingredients, and purée until smooth. Transfer the base into a smaller pitcher, and chill thoroughly for at least three hours before churning in your ice cream machine according to the manufacturer's directions. Transfer the soft ice cream to an airtight container and store it in the freezer for another three hours minimum, until frozen solid, before serving.

It would be impossible to talk of toasted marshmallows without giving s'mores, the most perfect application for those beautifully charred confections, a tip of the hat. Mix in 1/2 cup of crushed graham cracker pieces and 1/4 cup mini chocolate chips within the last five minutes of churning for a frozen version of the beloved s'more.

CHOCOLATE AND VANILLA

Black Pearl Ice Cream

Makes About
1 Quart

Discovering this unusual, Asian-inspired flavor combination was pure serendipity, but ever since trying it once, I can't seem to get it out of my head. The way that ginger and wasabi brighten up a dry, dark chocolate is a sensational pairing in itself, but it's the sesame seeds that are the real star here.

2 3/4 Cups Plain, Non-Dairy Milk
1/2 Cup Granulated Sugar
1/4 Cup Dark Brown Sugar, Firmly
Packed
1/2 Cup Toasted Black Sesame
Seeds

2 Tablespoons Dutch-Processed
Cocoa Powder
1 Tablespoon Cornstarch
1 Tablespoon Wasabi Paste
1 1/4 Teaspoons Ground Ginger
1/2 Teaspoon Instant Coffee Powder

1/8 Teaspoon Salt
Pinch Freshly Ground Black Pepper
(Optional)
2 Ounces (1/3 Cup) Semi-Sweet
Chocolate Chips

If you have a high-speed blender, you can just toss everything in, except for the chocolate chips, and let it go. Purée for one to two minutes on high, until completely smooth. Otherwise, if using a regular blender, place the black sesame seeds in the blender first, and grind them down to a fine powder, pausing to scrape down the sides of the canister as needed. Then you can go ahead and add the remaining ingredients except for the chocolate, blending thoroughly until smooth. Pass the mixture through a strainer to ensure a silky texture.

Pour the contents of your blender into a medium saucepan, and set over moderate heat. Whisk occasionally until the ice cream base has just begun to boil and has thickened significantly. This custard turns out a bit thicker than most, so you need to stay very close by at all times, scraping the sides and bottom of the pan to prevent sticking and burning. Remove from the heat and add in the chocolate, stirring continuously until it has melted from the residual heat. Cool completely.

Chill thoroughly before churning in your ice cream maker according to the manufacturer's instructions. Transfer to an airtight container and freeze solidly for at least three hours before serving.

Double Chocolate Fudge Chunk Ice Cream

Makes About
1 1/2 Quarts

What could make chocolate ice cream even better? Why, more chocolate, of course! Rather than tossing in the standard smattering of chips to bump up the cocoa quotient, or even marbling in a swirled syrupy ripple, this ice cream is enhanced by serious chunks of genuine fudge. Over time, the chunks soften in the freezer, melting down into gooey pockets of sweet chocolate nectar, so some might say that this one gets even better with age.

Chocolate Fudge Ice Cream:

2/3 Cup Granulated Sugar
2 Tablespoons Natural Cocoa
   Powder
2 Tablespoons Arrowroot

1/2 Teaspoon Instant Coffee
   Powder
1/4 Teaspoon Salt
3 Cups Plain, Non-Dairy Milk
3 Ounces (1/2 Cup) Semi-Sweet
   Chocolate Chips

Fast Fudge Chunks:

4 Ounces (2/3 Cup) Semi-Sweet
   Chocolate Chips
3 Tablespoons Non-Dairy Margarine
1/3 Cup Confectioner's Sugar
1/4 Teaspoon Vanilla Extract
Pinch Salt

In a large saucepan, combine the sugar, cocoa powder, arrowroot, coffee powder, and salt, whisking to distribute the dry ingredients evenly throughout. Pour in just about a 1/2 cup of the non-dairy milk, and whisk vigorously to form a thick paste, making sure to moisten all of the dry goods and get out any lumps. Once smooth and homogeneous, go ahead and add in the remaining non-dairy milk, and whisk until smooth. Turn on the stove to medium heat and whisk the mixture occasionally as it comes up to temperature. When you see bubbles just beginning to form around the edges, that's your cue to add in the chocolate chips.

Switch over to a wide spatula and stir gently, scraping the bottom and sides of the pan, to make sure that nothing sticks and that the chocolate fully melts. Once the mixture comes up to a full boil, cook for just a minute or two longer, and as long as there are no more whole chocolate chips remaining, turn off the heat. Let cool completely before moving it into the refrigerator to chill, about three hours.

To begin on the fudge chunks in the meantime, lightly grease a 4- x 8-inch loaf pan.

In a large bowl, combine the chocolate chips, sugar, and cocoa. In a small saucepan, place the margarine and coconut milk, and stir together over medium-low heat. Cook the mixture until the margarine has melted and bubbles just begin to break at the surface. Remove it from the stove and immediately pour over the chocolate mixture. Let everything sit for a couple of minutes; then stir vigorously to melt the chocolate and incorporate the dry ingredients. Continue stirring until the mixture is completely smooth—it may take some serious elbow grease to get all of the dry goods mixed in, but just keep at it! Everything will come together with time.

Stir in the vanilla and salt, and then quickly pour everything into your prepared pan. Smooth out the top with your spatula so that the fudge fills the bottom of the pan in an even layer. Chill for at least one hour for the fudge to fully solidify before cutting into small, bite-sized squares. Set aside in the freezer so that the pieces remain as cold as possible.

Churn the ice cream base in your machine according to the manufacturer's instructions. As you transfer spoonfuls of the soft ice cream to an airtight container, gently fold your fudge chunks into each addition. Give the whole thing a good mix to distribute the goodies throughout, and seal tightly before moving it to the freezer. Let solidify for at least four hours before serving.

French Vanilla Ice Cream

Makes
1 Scant Quart

After centuries of ice cream consumption, vanilla is still firmly situated at the top of the list, outselling chocolate almost 2:1. My take on this classic is pretty simple, but incredibly rich. High-quality vanilla beans are the key to this flavor, and while you could get by with using vanilla paste instead, plain old extract just doesn't cut it for me in this case. If you're unconvinced that vanilla is so special, just try this approach; it will change your mind!

2 Cups Plain, Non-Dairy Milk
1/4 Cup Bird's Custard Powder*
1/2 Cup Granulated Sugar

Pinch Salt
2 Whole Vanilla Beans or 2
    Tablespoons Vanilla Paste

3 Tablespoons Margarine or Coconut
    Oil

In a medium saucepan, whisk together the non-dairy milk, custard powder, sugar, and salt while the liquid is still cold, being sure to get out any clumps. Use a knife to split the vanilla beans down the middle and scrape out the seeds. Toss the seeds and spent pods, or vanilla paste, into the pan.

Set the mixture over medium heat, whisking continuously until it comes to a boil. Immediately turn off the heat, and carefully remove the pods. Don't throw them out; they can still be washed off, dried, and placed in a container of sugar to make vanilla sugar.

While the custard is still hot, whisk in the margarine and stir until it has fully melted and incorporated. Let chill completely in the refrigerator before proceeding.

The custard will be very thick once chilled, so be sure to whisk vigorously, or give it a quick spin in the blender before churning in your ice cream maker according to the manufacturer's instructions.

Transfer the soft ice cream into an airtight container, and let it rest in the freezer for at least three hours before serving, until solid enough to scoop.

*Custard powder mimics the flavor that eggs would traditionally provide, giving it that extra creamy decadence so hard to come by in commercial offerings. However, if you can't get your hands on it, an equal amount of cornstarch will work as well.

German Chocolate Ice Cream

Makes About
1 Quart

Chocoholics, rejoice! Premium chocolate ice cream can't hold a candle to this intense, decadent concoction. Better yet, it's not just plain old cocoa custard, but a marbled beauty, swirled through and through with sweet coconut flakes, much like the filling found in German chocolate cake. Despite the connotations, German chocolate cake doesn't hail from Germany, but is in fact the creation of Sam German, an American baker in the 1950s. Go ahead and really layer the coconut in for this ice cream—it's hard to imagine ending up with "too much," even if it looks like a lot compared to the ice cream base.

Chocolate Ice Cream:

1 1/2 Cups Dutch-Processed Cocoa Powder
1 Cup Granulated Sugar
1 Tablespoon Arrowroot Powder
1 Teaspoon Instant Coffee Powder
1/4 Teaspoon Salt
1/8 Teaspoon Ground Cinnamon
2 Cups Plain, Non-Dairy Milk

1 Teaspoon Vanilla Extract
1 12-Ounce Package Extra-Firm Silken Tofu
3 Ounces Semi-Sweet Chocolate, Melted

Coconut Swirl:

1/4 Cup Plain, Non-Dairy Milk
1 1/2 Teaspoons Arrowroot Powder

1/4 Cup Granulated Sugar
1/2 Tablespoon Margarine
1/2 Teaspoon Vanilla Extract
3/4 Cup Unsweetened Coconut Flakes
1/4 Cup Finely Chopped Pecans

To make the chocolate ice cream, begin by combining the cocoa, sugar, arrowroot powder, coffee powder, salt, and cinnamon in a medium saucepan. While whisking continuously, slowly pour in the non-dairy milk, and beat vigorously until there are no more lumps. Turn on the heat to medium and bring the mixture just to a boil, stirring gently the whole time to prevent the solids from settling on the bottom of the pot and burning. Remove from the heat and let cool for a few minutes.

Place the vanilla and tofu in your blender or food processor and thoroughly purée, scraping down the sides of the bowl as necessary. Once smooth, add in the melted chocolate, followed by the cooked chocolate custard, and pulse until the mixture is well blended and homogeneous. Chill thoroughly in the refrigerator.

For the coconut swirl, combine the non-dairy milk, arrowroot powder, and sugar together in a small saucepan over medium heat, making sure to get out all of the lumps. Cook just until bubbles begin to break on the surface; then turn off the heat. Quickly stir in the margarine so that it melts, followed by the vanilla, coconut, and pecans. Let cool while you begin to churn the ice cream in your ice cream maker according to the manufacturer's instructions.

Transfer the soft ice cream into an airtight container, layering scoops of ice cream with spoonfuls of the coconut swirl. Let it rest in the freezer for at least three hours before serving, until solid enough to scoop.

Gravel Path Ice Cream

Makes About
1 Quart

Agravel path is more inviting than a rocky road, easier to navigate, and in the case of this ice cream, so much more delicious. Packed full of tons of little mix-ins rather than just a few huge chunks, each bite brings new flavors and textures, with a far more sophisticated flavor profile than the original inspiration. Save the rocky road for tough times; celebrate the good in life with gravel path instead!

1/4 Cup Dutch-Processed Cocoa
    Powder
2/3 Cup Granulated Sugar
2 Tablespoons Cornstarch
1/2 Teaspoon Instant Coffee Powder
1/4 Teaspoon Salt

2 2/3 Cups Chocolate or Vanilla
    Non-Dairy Milk
1/2 Cup Roughly Chopped Vegan
    Marshmallows
1/4 Cup Unsweetened Cacao Nibs

1/4 Cup Mini Chocolate Chips, or
    Finely Chopped Semi-Sweet
    Chocolate
1/4 Cup Whole Toasted Almonds,
    Chopped
1/4 Cup Whole Toasted Cashews,
    Chopped

In a medium saucepan, whisk together the cocoa powder, sugar, cornstarch, coffee powder, and salt so that the mixture of dry goods is homogeneous. Pour in about 1/3 of the non-dairy milk, and whisk vigorously to create a thick paste, scrupulously scraping the bottom of the pan to beat out any potential lumps. The cocoa may resist blending at first, so be persistent! Once entirely smooth, slowly pour in the remaining non-dairy milk while continuing to whisk until all the liquid is incorporated.

Turn on the heat to medium, and whisk occasionally until the ice cream base comes up to a boil. Cook for a minute longer, carefully scraping the sides and bottom of the pan so that the custard doesn't burn; then turn off the heat. Cool completely before moving the base into your fridge to chill before churning, at least three hours.

Churn in your ice cream maker according to the manufacturer's instructions. While the ice cream spins, assemble your mix-ins. Chop and toss everything together, and set aside. Once the ice cream is ready, transfer spoonfuls into an airtight container, and sprinkle a handful of mix-ins over each new addition. Give the whole thing a good stir, from the bottom to the top of the container, to equally distribute all of the goodies throughout. Cover and move the soft ice cream into your freezer to fully solidify before serving; a minimum of another three hours.

Hint-of-Mint Chocolate Sorbet

Makes About
1 Quart

An intense rush of pure chocolate flavor, combined with a subtle, refreshing essence of mint, this rich sorbet is deceptively light but still full-bodied and entirely satisfying—it's the ideal dessert to cap off a hot summer's day. This is hands-down my favorite use for extra fresh mint, since it comes together so effortlessly and is always a huge crowd-pleaser.

3 Cups Water
1 Ounce Fresh Mint Leaves,*
   Roughly Chopped and Bruised
1 1/3 Cups Granulated Sugar

1 Cup Dutch-Processed Cocoa
   Powder
1 Teaspoon Vanilla Extract

1/2 Teaspoon Salt
3 Ounces Dark Chocolate, Finely
   Chopped

Combine the water and fresh mint in a small saucepan and bring to a boil. Immediately turn off the heat, cover with the lid, and let infuse for forty-five to sixty minutes. Strain, pressing all of the liquid out of the mint, and discard the spent leaves.

Combine 1/3 cup of the mint water and all of the sugar in a medium saucepan over medium-high heat. Stir just to combine; then keep that spatula away at this stage of the game. As the mixture cooks, the sugar will dissolve and eventually come to a boil. Continue cooking, swirling the pan occasionally to mix the contents, about eight to twelve minutes, until the sugar turns a golden caramel color. Add the remaining water carefully, standing back in case of splashing. The caramel will seize and sputter a bit; don't worry if it appears to harden. Cook gently once again until the caramel is dissolved, immediately removing the pot from the heat once smooth. Thoroughly whisk in the cocoa powder, vanilla, and salt, making sure there are absolutely no lumps. Finally, add in the chocolate, and whisk until fully melted and the whole mixture is perfectly smooth.

Chill thoroughly, for at least three hours, before freezing in your ice cream maker per the manufacturer's instructions. Once churned, pack the sorbet into an airtight container and freeze solidly before serving. This sorbet turns out a bit softer than most, so it will take nearly a full day to become scoopable; it's quite delightful as more of a soft serve consistency too, though.

*Plain peppermint or spearmint leaves are equally refreshing, but if you're fond of gardening, consider adding a specialty mint variety to your herb lineup. We don't get enough sunlight to grow much, but mint is a particularly hardy plant that has a propensity to take over any plot of earth once it takes root. I specifically grow black peppermint for its clean, sweet, and bright flavor. The fine nuances of some boutique varieties like pineapple mint, lemon mint, and ginger mint may become lost in a complex dessert, but anything vaguely minty can absolutely work.

Hot Chocolate Ice Cream

Makes About
1 Quart

Calling any sort of ice cream "hot" is a bit of a misnomer, I suppose, but forget the temperature connotations and consider the decadent, wintery drink. Rich, bitter chocolate coats the tongue and fills the belly, but fluffy, gooey marshmallows add lightness and balance to the whole concoction brilliantly. This combination is so dangerously addictive, you may find yourself headed to the freezer instead of the stove come chillier months!

2 1/2 Cups Chocolate Non-Dairy
    Milk
1 Ounce Unsweetened Baker's
    Chocolate, Roughly Chopped

3/4 Cup Granulated Sugar
1/4 Cup Natural Cocoa Powder
2 Tablespoons Arrowroot
1 Teaspoon Maca Powder (Optional)

1/4 Teaspoon Salt
1 Teaspoon Vanilla Extract
3/4 Cup Chopped Vegan
    Marshmallows

In a medium saucepan, warm the chocolate "milk" over moderate heat, and add in the chopped chocolate. Whisk occasionally to make sure that the chocolate pieces don't just settle to the bottom and burn, until completely melted and smooth. Meanwhile, combine the sugar, cocoa, arrowroot, maca, and salt in a separate dish, and stir well to evenly distribute all of the dry goods throughout. Once the chocolate "milk" mixture on the stove is smooth and creamy again, slowly sift in the dry ingredients, whisking vigorously to break up any clumps that may form. Continue to cook gently, stirring every few minutes, until the mixture comes to a boil and has thickened in consistency. Remove from the heat before introducing the vanilla. Let cool to room temperature before moving the base into your fridge to chill, for at least one hour. Once the chocolatey base is nice and cold, process in your ice cream maker according to the manufacturer's instructions, adding the chopped marshmallows in the last five minutes or so of churning.

Transfer the soft ice cream into an airtight container, and let rest in the freezer for at least three hours before serving, until solid enough to scoop.

> Turn up the heat, and transform this concoction into a Mexican Hot Chocolate Ice Cream with just a few spicy additions. Incorporate 1 teaspoon ground cinnamon, 1/4 teaspoon ground cayenne pepper, 1/4 teaspoon chili powder, and a pinch of freshly ground black pepper into the base, and churn as instructed.

Midnight Munchies Ice Cream

Makes
1–1 1/2 Quarts

In an attempt to appease an insatiable midnight munchies appetite, I dreamed up what I would most crave as a midnight snack. Ice cream naturally came to mind first, and it had to be a most indulgent flavor, satisfying both my sweet tooth and my propensity toward salty snacks all in one spoonful. Creamy chocolate ice cream and potato chip toffee, together in a harmonious marriage at last.

Chocolate Ice Cream Base:

1/2 Cup Granulated Sugar
1/4 Cup Dark Brown Sugar, Firmly
    Packed
1/4 Cup Black Cocoa Powder
1 1/2 Tablespoons Cornstarch
1/4 Teaspoon Salt
2 1/2 Cups Plain, Non-Dairy Milk

3 Ounces (1/2 Cup) Semi-Sweet
    Chocolate Chips
1 Teaspoon Vanilla Extract

Potato Chip Toffee:

6 Tablespoons Non-Dairy Margarine

2 Ounces (2 Heaping Cups) Thick-
    cut Potato Chips,* Lightly
    Crushed
2/3 Cup Granulated Sugar
2 Teaspoons Apple Cider Vinegar
2 Ounces (1/3 Cup) Semi-Sweet
    Chocolate Chips

Beginning with the ice cream base, whisk together both sugars, cocoa, cornstarch, and salt in a medium saucepan, breaking up the brown sugar to the best of your ability, and making sure that the dry goods are well combined. Pour in about a 1/4 cup of the non-dairy milk to create a thick paste, whisking vigorously to beat out any clumps. Once smooth, add the remainder of the "milk."

Set over medium heat and whisk occasionally until the mixture comes to a boil. Add in the chocolate chips and reduce the heat to medium-low, stirring constantly until the chocolate has completely melted. Take care to scrape the bottom and sides of the pan to prevent any sticking and burning. Immediately turn off the heat when smooth and thickened in consistency, and finally whisk in the vanilla. Let cool to room temperature before chilling; chill for at least three hours before churning.

In preparation for the toffee, line a baking sheet with a silpat or parchment paper. Place the potato chips in a large bowl and lightly crush them with a potato masher. You don't want tiny crumbs, but pieces about the size of sliced almonds so that you can more easily incorporate them into the candy. Set aside.

In a medium saucepan, combine the margarine, sugar, and vinegar. Set over medium-low heat just until the margarine has melted and you can fully incorporate the sugar into the mixture. Turn up to medium, and bring it to a vigorous boil. Cook until the sugar has dissolved and slowly becomes a deep golden color. A candy thermometer should read somewhere around 300–310 degrees, otherwise known as the hard-crack stage; this should take ten to fifteen minutes.

Remove from the heat and fold in your crushed chips. Immediately pour the hot toffee onto your prepared baking sheet and press out into a fairly thin layer. Let cool completely.

Melt the chocolate either in a double-boiler or in the microwave, zapping at thirty-second intervals. Stir well until entirely smooth. Smother your toffee with the melted chocolate, spreading it out to coat the top. There are no points for neatness here, so go ahead and just smear it on. Let cool again so that the chocolate completely hardens; then chop roughly into bite-sized chunks. Set aside in a cool, dry place until you're ready to mix it into your ice cream. For longer-term storage, stash the pieces in an airtight container.

Churn the ice cream base according to the instructions provided by your ice cream machine's manufacturer. Mix in generous handfuls of potato chip toffee as you pack the soft ice cream into an airtight container; use a wide spatula to fold in as much toffee as you can stuff in there, but anticipate having some leftover to use as a topping or for snacking separately. Let solidify in the freezer for at least three hours before serving. Eaten within the first five to seven days, the toffee will still have a sturdy crunch, but will soften over time into delightful caramel-like puddles.

*Seek out kettle-style chips, which tend to be heartier and thicker than other styles, so that the earthy potato flavor and crunchy texture can hold up a toffee coating.

Mouse Tracks Ice Cream

**Makes About
1 1/2 Quarts**

Confusion over the origins of the name "moose tracks" can be excused with just one glance at this swirled and speckled flavor, absolutely stuffed to the brim with sweet buried treasures. A rich, custard-like base holds on to a river of gooey fudge, and huge pieces of chopped peanut butter cups add a nutty crunch. Since the original name makes so little sense, I like to believe that my modification to "mouse tracks" is a fittingly inexplicable alteration.

Custard Base:

3 Tablespoons Bird's Custard Powder
   or Cornstarch
2/3 Cup Granulated Sugar
3 Tablespoons Dark Brown Sugar,
   Firmly Packed
1 1/2 Teaspoons Natural Cocoa Powder
1/8 Teaspoon Salt
2 3/4 Cup Plain, Non-Dairy Milk
1 Tablespoon Vanilla Extract

Peanut Butter Cup Chunks:

4 Ounces (2/3 Cup) Semi-Sweet
   Chocolate Chips, Divided
1 Teaspoon Coconut Oil, Divided
1/2 Cup Creamy Peanut Butter
1/4 Cup Confectioner's Sugar
Splash Vanilla Extract
1/8 Teaspoon Salt

Fudge Ripple:

1/2 Cup Granulated Sugar
1/4 Cup Light Corn Syrup or Agave
   Nectar
1/4 Cup Water
1/3 Cup Dutch-Processed Cocoa
   Powder
Pinch Salt

If making this ice cream all in one shot, begin by making the custard so that it has time to cool. In a medium saucepan, combine the custard powder, both sugars, cocoa, and salt. Pour in about 1/3 cup of the non-dairy milk and work the dry goods into a thick paste, taking care to get out all the lumps. Once smooth, whisk in the remaining non-dairy milk and turn on the heat to medium. Bring the mixture up to a boil, whisking occasionally, and then let cook for two to three minutes longer for the custard powder to reach its full thickening potential. Turn off the heat, cool, and then chill thoroughly in the fridge.

> Though the multiple components take a bit more effort to assemble than a more straightforward ice cream recipe, it's all very simple stuff. Make the short-cut peanut butter cup chunks, molded as one flat rectangle rather than finicky individual rounds, and fudge ripple up to a week in advance to save time.

The peanut butter cup is made in one single sheet, rather than numerous little candies, for ease of preparation. What's the sense in carefully molding pieces that are only going to get chopped up and mashed into ice cream anyway?

Save yourself the hassle and pull out an 8- x 4-inch loaf pan. Line it with aluminum foil, carefully pressing it flat against the sides and into the corners before lightly greasing. Set aside.

Combine half of the chocolate and half of the coconut oil in a microwave-safe dish, and heat for just thirty seconds. Stir very well, and if all of the pieces aren't entirely melted, microwave for an additional fifteen to thirty seconds. Stir again until completely smooth. Pour the liquid chocolate into your prepared pan and tilt it all around so that the chocolate fully coats the bottom. Stash it on a flat area in the freezer for set up—it should only take about ten minutes or so to solidify.

Meanwhile, mash together the peanut butter, confectioner's sugar, vanilla, and salt thoroughly, until smooth. A stand mixer will speed up the process, but isn't necessary. Spread out the peanut butter filling in an even layer on top of the chocolate.

Melt the remaining chocolate and coconut oil as per the previous instructions, and pour that on top of the peanut butter. Use your spatula to carefully ease it over the top, so that it completely covers the filling. Return the whole pan to the freezer to set up. After about thirty minutes, flip the giant peanut butter cup out onto a cutting board and peel away the foil. Chop it roughly into chunks, and don't be alarmed if the chocolate coating cracks away in some places. It doesn't need to look beautiful, because it will taste delicious no matter what!

For the fudge ripple, whisk all of the ingredients vigorously and thoroughly in a small saucepan, beating the mixture until all of the dry goods are incorporated. The cocoa especially will resist blending, but be persistent and it will all smooth out. Place over medium-low heat, bring to a boil; then reduce the heat slightly so that it boils for a full minute. Immediately remove from the heat and cool before refrigerating until ready to use. The resulting fudge sauce will continue to thicken a bit as it cools.

Churn the custard base into your ice cream maker according to the manufacturer's instructions. Spoon about one-third of the finished but still-soft ice cream into an airtight container, sprinkle with a third of the peanut butter cup chunks, and drizzle randomly with a third of the fudge ripple. Repeat with the remaining components, working as quickly as possible so that the ice cream doesn't melt, until everything is packed into your container. Stash it in the freezer for at least four hours to set up before serving.

Naked Frozen Yogurt

Makes 1 Scant Quart

No funny business, no fancy flavors, just full-frontal frozen yogurt. Use this luscious frozen-yogurt base as the starting point for limitless dessert possibilities, or simply enjoy with fresh fruit toppings for a fun way to enjoy a healthy yogurt treat. For a more decadent experience, pile your swirled mountains of freshly churned and still-soft frozen yogurt high with chocolate sauce (page 204), sprinkles (page 212), mochi bites (page 208) chopped nuts—Anything goes!

3 Cups Plain, Unsweetened Vegan
   Yogurt

2/3 Cup Light Agave Nectar
1 Teaspoon Vanilla (Optional)

Line a fine mesh strainer with cheesecloth and fill with yogurt. Wrap the edges of the cheesecloth over the yogurt until fully covered, and place strainer over a pot deep enough to catch the liquid and keep the yogurt from sitting in the moisture. Cover the whole pot and strainer with plastic wrap, allowing it to sit and drain in the refrigerator for twenty-four to thirty-six hours. The amount of liquid released will vary by brand, but the key is that the yogurt will become a bit thicker and more concentrated.

In a medium bowl, combine the strained yogurt, agave, and vanilla if using. Churn in your ice cream machine per the manufacturer's instructions. For a soft-serve consistency, serve immediately after freezing. For a firmer consistency more like standard ice cream, pack into an airtight container and let solidify in the freezer for at least four hours.

> Any flavor you can imagine can seamlessly slip into this recipe. For starters, try a coffee variation by blending in 1 tablespoon of instant coffee powder before churning. One teaspoon of matcha will create a pleasantly bitter green tea treat. Enrich things a bit with 1/2 cup of peanut butter, sure to be a hit with those nutcases among us. A 1/3 cup of Dutch-processed cocoa powder can create a light chocolatey flavor that still allows the yogurt base to shine. Get in there and mix things up—it's hard to go wrong with this foolproof base.

Super-Simple Chocolate Kefir Ice Cream

Makes
1 Scant Quart

Tangy and tart like frozen yogurt but with a deep cocoa kick, this probiotic power snack is as easy as picking up a whisk. Leading with a sophisticated, slightly bitter edge, the complexity of its flavor profile is impressive for a combination of just four ingredients. Fermented with healthy bacteria like yogurt, commercial vegan kefir is typically made from rich coconut milk, and reminds me of buttermilk.

2 1/2 Cups Plain Coconut Kefir*   3/4 Cup Agave Nectar
1 Cup Natural Cocoa Powder   1/4 Teaspoon Salt

Simply whisk everything together vigorously until smooth, and chill if not already cold. Churn according to the instructions provided by your specific ice cream machine. Transfer the finished ice cream to an airtight container and let further solidify in the freezer for at least six hours before serving.

*Though fairly common in U.S. health food stores, coconut kefir is still a relative rarity elsewhere. Alternately, you can also use 2 cups plain vegan yogurt or "sour cream" plus 1/2 cup plain, non-dairy milk.

Toffee Crunch Ice Cream

Makes About
1 Quart

Sweet toffee and bitter cacao nibs both lend their own distinctive crunch to this buttery vanilla ice cream. This will make more toffee than you need for the ice cream itself, but you shouldn't have much of a problem finding other ways to enjoy it. I like to garnish the finished, frozen scoops with a few generous wedges of toffee on top, although it's also quite tempting to eat all by itself.

Vanilla Ice Cream Base:

2 1/2 Cups Plain, Non-Dairy Milk
2/3 Cup Granulated Sugar
2 Tablespoons Cornstarch
1 1/2 Teaspoons Arrowroot
1/2 Teaspoon Nutritional Yeast

1/4 Teaspoon Salt
1 Tablespoon Non-Dairy Margarine
2 Teaspoons Vanilla Extract

Toffee:

1/2 Cup Non-Dairy Margarine

1 Cup Granulated Sugar
Pinch Salt
4 Ounces (2/3 Cup) Semi-Sweet
    Chocolate Chips
1 Ounce Dark Chocolate-Covered
    Cacao Nibs

In a medium saucepan, combine the non-dairy milk, sugar, cornstarch, arrowroot, nutritional yeast, and salt. Beat thoroughly before turning on the heat to break up all lumps, big and small. Turn the flame up to medium and whisk occasionally, until the mixture comes to a boil. Let cook at a full boil for two additional minutes, and then remove the pan from the burner. Add in the margarine and vanilla extract, stirring to incorporate and allowing the residual heat to melt the margarine. Let cool to room temperature, and then chill thoroughly for at least three hours before churning.

Meanwhile, start up the toffee by laying out a silpat or piece of parchment paper near the stove. Combine the margarine, sugar, and salt in a medium saucepan, and set it on the stove over medium-low heat just until the margarine has melted and you can fully incorporate the sugar into the mixture. Turn up to medium, and bring it to a vigorous boil. Cook until the sugar has dissolved and slowly becomes a deep golden color. A candy thermometer should read somewhere around 300–310 degrees, otherwise known as the hard-crack stage, and should take ten to fifteen minutes.

Remove from the heat and immediately pour the hot toffee onto your prepared baking sheet. It should spread out naturally, so there's no need to push it around with a spatula. Let cool completely. Melt the chocolate, and then pour it on top of the hardened toffee, smoothing it out in an even layer. Allow the chocolate to solidify in a cool spot for at least two hours before breaking or chopping the toffee roughly. Set aside.

Churn ice cream base in your ice cream machine according to the manufacturer's directions. In the last five minutes of churning, slowly sprinkle the cacao nibs right into the machine, so that the moving paddle incorporates and distributes the pieces throughout the ice cream. Transfer dollops of the soft ice cream to an airtight container, scattering pieces of toffee over each addition. Stir everything together thoroughly and store it in the freezer for another three hours minimum, or until frozen solid, before serving.

Vanilla Bean "Honey" Ice Cream

**Makes About
1 Quart**

While I'm sure that many people would write off such a combination for being too plain, the delicate nuances of vanilla bean and honey flavors are so clean and pure, they simply come alive. Happy to share the spotlight, this is the flavor I first think to pair with a more elaborate dessert, like a pie or cake, since it provides an agreeable foil to nearly everything else.

3 Cups Plain Vegan Creamer
2 Tablespoons Arrowroot

3/4 Cup Vegan "Honey" Syrup (page 224) or Honey-Flavored Agave Nectar

1 Whole Vanilla Bean, Split and Seeds Scraped
Pinch Salt

In a medium saucepan, vigorously whisk together the creamer and arrowroot so that there are no lumps of starch remaining. Set the pan over moderate heat, and add in the "honey" and vanilla bean seeds. Whisk occasionally, until it just comes to a boil, and the liquid has thickened significantly. Turn off the heat and let cool. Chill for at least three hours, and then churn in your ice cream maker according to the manufacturer's instructions. Pack into an airtight container and store in the freezer.

A classic combination that always comes to mind when thinking about honey is the Rosh Hashanah favorite of apples and honey. This pairing is ideal for all sorts of dessert spin-offs, and ice cream is no exception. Peel, core, and chop one medium-sized sweet apple and sauté over medium heat with 1 tablespoon non-dairy margarine and 3 tablespoons dark brown sugar, firmly packed. Cook until the apples are tender, let cool completely, and chill. Fold the apple swirl in after the ice cream is done churning. Do the delicate nuances of vegan "honey" get lost on you? Try something a bit more bold and decadent, like salted butterscotch ice cream! Just replace the "honey" with an equal measure of butterscotch sauce (page 196) plus an extra pinch of coarse sea salt over each serving.

White Chocolate Ice Cream

Makes About
1 Quart

Pure as freshly fallen snow and delicious in its own right, simply avoid the stuff with milk solids, waxy hydrogenated fats, and artificial flavors, and you'll find an entirely different white chocolate experience awaits you. The biggest stumbling block to universal white chocolate acceptance is that tasters expect the stuff to be similar to all other sorts of chocolates, whereas it's a unique experience in its own right. Paired with supple, aromatic vanilla beans, there's hardly a more decadent flavor to be found.

6 Ounces (1/2 Package) Extra-Firm
   Silken Tofu
2 1/2 Cups Plain, Non-Dairy Milk
1 1/2 Tablespoons Arrowroot

3/4 Cup Light Agave Nectar
1/4 Teaspoon Salt
1 Whole Vanilla Bean, Split and
   Scraped

2–3 Ounces Vegan White Chocolate,
   Finely Chopped,* Homemade
   (page 225) or Store-Bought

Toss your tofu, non-dairy milk, arrowroot, agave, and salt into your blender, and purée to a silky-smooth consistency. Transfer to a medium saucepan, and set over medium heat on the stove. Scrape the seeds of the vanilla bean into the mixture, and stir well. Bring to a full boil, stirring occasionally; then reduce the heat to low. Add the white chocolate, and stir constantly until it all completely melts. Turn off the heat immediately, and let cool. Refrigerate for at least three hours, until thoroughly chilled.

Churn in your ice cream machine according to the manufacturer's directions. Transfer the soft ice cream to an airtight container, and store it in the freezer for another three hours minimum, until frozen solid, before serving.

> Dreaming of a white Christmas? Soak 1/2 cup of dried cranberries in 1/4 cup of rum overnight, and then within the final five minutes of churning the white chocolate base, mix them in along with 1/4 cup of chopped green pistachios. The red and green polka dots make for a festive treat!

Be sure to let this particular ice cream thaw and "warm" a bit before eating, because the higher proportion of cocoa butter in white chocolate can sometimes lead to a grainier texture when frozen. The mixture feels smoother on the tongue when it's less frozen, and the particles of cocoa butter dissolve more readily at body temperature.

*There's a variable amount of white chocolate listed here, because it depends on whether you purchase ready-made chips or make it yourself. One batch homemade produces just over 2 ounces when made according to the recipe on page 225 which will suffice, but the greater measure is more appropriate if using store-bought.

COFFEE, TEA, OR ME: LIBATIONS

Bloody Mary Ice Cream

Makes
1–1 1/2 Quarts

Savory ice cream? You bet! More of a palate-cleanser than a dessert, this bright, punchy tomato elixir will snap you out of a dull dinner and leave you feeling invigorated. A decent punch of alcohol makes up for the lack of sugar and keeps this little number smooth and creamy. Like the standard brunch staple, the exact mix is largely up to interpretation and personal tastes, so feel free to ramp up (or down) the spices as desired.

2 1/2 Cups Plain Vegan Creamer
2 6-Ounce Cans Tomato Paste
3 Tablespoons Lemon Juice
1 Tablespoon Light Agave Nectar

1 Tablespoon Vegan Worcestershire
  Sauce* or Soy Sauce
1 Teaspoon Hot Sauce
Pinch Ground Black Pepper
1/2 Teaspoon Celery Seed

1/2 Teaspoon Salt
3 Tablespoons Cornstarch
1/2 Cup Vodka

Combine all the ingredients in your blender and purée until smooth. Pass through a strainer to ensure a flawlessly creamy texture; then chill for at least an hour before churning in your ice cream machine according to the manufacturer's suggestions. Transfer to an airtight container and stash in the freezer for at least four hours to solidify before serving.

For an extra flourish, garnish scoops with celery sticks and/or lemon wedges if desired.

*Anchovies are a sneaky addition that often find their way into this mysterious savory sauce, so be vigilant about reading the ingredients list before making your purchase. Unfortunately, most mainstream brands couldn't care less about throwing in a few stinky fishes, so keep an eye out for specifically vegan labels, such as Annie's® or The Wizard's® Worcestershire sauce.

Chai Latte Ice Cream

Makes About
1 Quart

Coffee and chai tea are two of my favorite beverages, hot or cold, so why not combine them into one frozen concoction? Strong as a double espresso, and then some perhaps, you may not want to have a scoop before bed, but it will definitely keep you wide awake (and refreshed) during the dog days of summer!

1 Cup Full-Fat Coconut Milk
1 Cup Plain, Non-Dairy Milk
1/3 Cup Ground Coffee Beans
1 1/2 Whole Star Anise
12 Whole Cloves
1/4 Teaspoon Ground Allspice

2 Whole Cinnamon Sticks, Broken in Half
1 Inch Fresh Ginger, Peeled and Roughly Chopped
15 Whole Black Peppercorns
1/2 Teaspoon Ground Cardamom

1/4 Teaspoon Salt
1 12-Ounce Package Extra-Firm Silken Tofu
2/3 Cup Agave Nectar
1 Teaspoon Vanilla Extract

In a medium saucepan, combine the coconut milk, non-dairy milk, ground coffee, all of the spices, and salt. Turn the heat up to medium, and bring the mixture just to the verge of boiling. Shut off the heat, cover your pan, and let steep for twenty to thirty minutes.

Meanwhile, toss the tofu into your food processor or blender and purée, scraping down the sides of the bowl as needed. Add in the agave and vanilla; then pulse until smooth and fully incorporated.

Strain your coconut and soy mixture using a coffee filter or a very fine mesh strainer, and extract as much liquid as possible out of the coffee grounds. Discard the used grounds and spices.

Transfer the liquid into your tofu mix and pulse to incorporate. Once homogeneous, chill the mixture for at least one hour in the refrigerator, and then churn it in your ice cream maker according to the manufacturer's instructions.

Transfer the soft ice cream into an airtight container, and let rest in the freezer for at least three hours before serving, until solid enough to scoop.

> Versatile to a fault, this is actually three recipes in one. By simply omitting either all of the spices, or the ground coffee, you can create plain coffee or chai ice cream, respectively.

Cherry Cola Ice Cream

Makes About
1 Quart

Fizzy, sweet, and refreshing, it's not just sodas that have all the fun anymore! Though not as effervescent, this frozen treat is much more invigorating than a few cool sips of a plain, old cola drink, with fresh cherries brightening the flavor profile far more than any artificial extracts ever could.

8 Cups Cola (NOT Diet)
2 1/2 Cups (12 Ounces) Pitted
   Cherries, Fresh or Frozen

1/2 Cup Full-Fat Coconut Milk
1/3 Cup Granulated Sugar
1 Teaspoon Vanilla Extract

Pinch Salt

Place the cola in a large saucepan, and set it on the stove over medium heat. Allow it to simmer steadily (not boil) until reduced to 1 cup. Be patient—this will take over an hour! After you finally get the cola down to just 1 cup of liquid, let it cool before proceeding.

In your food processor or blender, combine the reduced cola, cherries (thawed, if using frozen), coconut milk, sugar, vanilla, and salt. Thoroughly purée until completely smooth; then pass the mixture through a strainer, if desired.

Let cool for at least one hour in the refrigerator before churning in your ice cream maker according to the manufacturer's instructions.

Transfer the soft ice cream into an airtight container, and let it rest in the freezer for at least three hours before serving, until solid enough to scoop.

If cola isn't your racket, don't let that stop you from making a fun, soda-inspired ice cream. For example, ginger ale or cream soda would make a fantastic accompaniment to ripe cherries as well!

Chocolate-Cabernet Ice Cream

Makes 1 Quart

Cabernet Sauvignon, bold and full-bodied yet often fruity and relatively sweet, is my perpetual top pick for a dessert wine. Not a wine to serve with dessert as that would typically imply—rather a wine to incorporate into dessert! Cabernet works nicely for both courses, but has a certain affinity for the slightly bitter, woodsy flavor profile of dark chocolate. The wine isn't cooked at all in this ice cream to preserve its signature assertive kick.

2 1/2 Cups Plain, Non-Dairy Milk
1 Tablespoon Arrowroot
2/3 Cup Granulated Sugar
1/4 Cup Dutch-Processed Cocoa
    Powder

Pinch Salt
3 Ounces (1/2 Cup) Dark Chocolate,
    Finely Chopped
3/4 Cup Cabernet Sauvignon, or Any
    Fruity Red Wine

1 Teaspoon Vanilla Extract

Combine the non-dairy milk, arrowroot, sugar, cocoa, and salt in a medium saucepan, and whisk vigorously until smooth. Be sure to beat out any lumps to ensure a silky-smooth ice cream later on. It may take a bit of time to incorporate all of the cocoa, so be patient and persistent. Turn on the heat to medium, and cook, whisking occasionally, until the mixture comes up to a full boil.

Reduce the heat to low, and add in the chopped chocolate. Whisk slowly but continuously until the chocolate pieces have completely melted and the whole ice cream base is perfectly smooth. Remove the saucepan from the heat and whisk in the wine and vanilla. Cool to room temperature before chilling for at least three hours in the fridge.

Churn in your ice cream maker according to the manufacturer's instructions. Transfer the soft ice cream to an airtight container, and let solidify in the freezer for at least six hours before serving.

Cookies 'n' Nog Ice Cream

Makes about
1 1/2 Quarts

Cookies and "egg" nog, frozen and fit for Santa Claus himself! Based upon my pistachio nog from Vegan Desserts, these leftovers became even greater than their original format after a quick spin through the ice cream machine. Gingery chunks of classic holiday cookies pepper this rich, creamy concoction, redolent with the aroma of ground nutmeg. Even snowy weather can't diminish the appeal of this festive, frozen combination. Who's to say that ice cream consumption should be limited to just the warmer seasons, anyway?

1/4 Cup Raw Pistachios
1/2 Cup Raw Cashews
1/2 Cup Unsalted Macadamia Nuts
3 Cups Plain, Non-Dairy Milk
2/3 Cup Light Agave Nectar

2 Tablespoons Arrowroot
3 Tablespoons Rum
1 Teaspoon Vanilla Extract
1/2 Teaspoon Ground Nutmeg
Pinch Ground Cinnamon

Pinch Black Salt
1 1/2–2 Cups Roughly Chopped Soft
   Ginger Cookies (page 214)

If using a high-speed blender, pile everything for the ice cream base from the pistachios to the salt into the container and let it rip on high. Thoroughly purée, until completely smooth, pausing to scrape down the sides if needed. Give it at least two to four minutes to ensure there are no gritty particles of the nuts remaining.

If using a standard blender, first soak all three nuts in ample cold water for at least six hours or overnight. This will soften them and encourage them to blend more readily, even in a machine with lower power. Thoroughly drain the nuts and pat them dry to remove as much excess water as possible. Toss them into the container of your blender, along with all of the remaining ingredients for the ice cream base, up to and including the salt. Thoroughly purée, pausing to scrape down the sides of the container periodically, until completely smooth. Allow somewhere around six to eight minutes to achieve a silky texture.

For both approaches, pass the base through a fine mesh strainer to remove any tricky pieces that may not have been blended. Chill the mixture thoroughly, for at least three hours in your fridge, before churning.

Churn according to your ice cream maker's instructions. Scoop spoonfuls of the fresh ice cream into an airtight container, and layer each addition with a generous sprinkling of chopped ginger cookies. Stir everything in the container once through to ensure even distribution. Quickly cover and stash in your freezer for at least three hours to solidify before serving. For an extra flourish, top scoops with an additional pinch of ground nutmeg!

Green Smoothie Ice Cream

Makes About
1 1/2 Quarts

Ice cream made with kale? Yes, it's true, and it's truly delicious, too! Super-powered whole food ingredients mean that this ice cream isn't a guilty indulgence in the least, but manages to bridge the gap from health food to comfort food. The key is to blend those greens very thoroughly, unless you plan on flossing your teeth with those plant fibers later on. This ice cream may sound like a wild stretch of the imagination, but the sum of these austere elements just might create a whole new health food craze.

6–8 Ounces Fresh Greens such as Spinach, Pea Shoots, Kale, Collards, Chard, etc.

2 Large, Ultra-Ripe Bananas (About 1 Pound with Peel)
1 1/2 Cups Full-Fat Coconut Milk
1 Cup Plain, Non-Dairy Milk

1 Tablespoon Cornstarch
1/2 Cup Diced Pineapple, Fresh or Frozen and Thawed
3/4 Cup Light Agave Nectar

Having a high-speed blender isn't strictly necessary, but it certainly makes things much easier for this recipe. Blending greens down to a smooth consistency can be tricky even with a sturdy standard model, so be prepared to blend for up to ten minutes and strain very carefully after processing if you go a lower-tech route.

Toss all of the greens, bananas, and 1 cup of the coconut milk into the container of your machine, in that order. It may seem like a ton of vegetation, but I promise it will blend down to a more manageable volume. Purée on high speed, pausing to scrape down the sides of the container as needed, until completely smooth. Then blend for another minute or so, because those fibrous greens always look much smoother than they feel on the tongue. Pass the mixture through a fine mesh sieve and set aside.

In a medium saucepan over medium heat, combine the remaining coconut milk, non-dairy milk, and cornstarch, whisking vigorously to combine and break up all possible clumps of starch. Add in the pineapple pieces and agave and bring to a boil. Cook for two more minutes; then turn off the heat. Transfer the mixture to your cleaned blender, and purée. Let cool completely before whisking both liquids together, mixing until homogeneous. Chill thoroughly in your refrigerator before churning.

Once ice-cold, churn the base in your ice cream machine according to the manufacturer's recommendations. Transfer to an airtight container when finished, and let rest in the freezer for at least three hours before serving.

Horchata Ice Cream

Makes
1–1 1/2 Quarts

Long before anyone thought those humble grains might produce a beverage to replace dairy, Mexican and Spanish cooks were churning out thick, rich drinks based on ground rice and sometimes almonds. Every mom and grandma has their own unique brew, often utilizing cinnamon and switching out the almonds for other nuts, but, naturally, a more popular addition is typically booze. Any sort will do, but keeping true to its origins, I prefer to use rum.

1/2 Cup Raw, Long Grain White Rice
3/4 Cup Raw, Whole Almonds
2 1/4 Cups Plain, Non-Dairy Milk
1 Cup Granulated Sugar

1 Teaspoon Ground Cinnamon
1/4 Teaspoon Salt
1/4 Cup Dark Rum, Grand Marnier,
    or Vodka*

1 1/2 Teaspoons Vanilla Extract
1/4 Teaspoon Almond Extract

Thoroughly rinse the rice, and place it in a spacious container along with the almonds. Cover with a generous amount of cold water, and let the two soak for a bare minimum of six hours, but ideally twelve to twenty-four. This will help soften those otherwise hard ingredients and allow them to blend more readily.

Drain the rice and almonds very well, removing as much water as possible, and transfer them into your blender. Add in the non-dairy milk, sugar, cinnamon, and salt. Purée, until the mixture is as smooth as possible. Depending on the power of your blender, this may take between four and ten minutes. There will likely still be a fine grit remaining, but don't worry about that. Pass the mixture through a fine mesh strainer lined with cheesecloth to catch any of the unblended solids. Discard the solids and transfer the smooth liquid to a medium saucepan.

Cook gently, over medium-low heat, stirring often and scraping the bottom of the pot to make sure that nothing sticks and burns. Bring the mixture just to the cusp of boiling, with bubbles beginning to break on the surface; then remove the pot from the heat. Mix in your spirit of choice and both extracts. Let cool completely, and chill for at least four hours before churning. The base will continue to thicken as it cools, becoming more viscous than many other ice creams at this stage.

Churn according to the instructions provided by your ice cream machine's manufacturer. Transfer to an airtight container when finished, and let freeze solid for at least three hours before serving.

*Each spirited option will contribute its own unique flavor (or lack thereof) depending on your preference. Straight-forward horchata typically doesn't include alcohol, but as an undeniably compatible mixer, it's hard to resist spiking this brew. Omit at your own risk; this ice cream freezes rather hard without it.

Matcha Ice Cream

Makes About
1 Quart

Food doesn't play a huge role in the Japanese tea ceremony, but like every other aspect, it's very important. Matcha is intensely strong and bitter, so it's always followed with a small plate of tiny, beautifully colored and painstakingly-shaped sweets, often filled with sweetened adzuki beans. Combining the drink with the dessert creates a harmony of flavors, which is what this ice cream strives for as well.

2 Cups Plain, Non-Dairy Milk
3/4 Cup Light Agave Nectar
1 1/2 Tablespoons Arrowroot
1 1/2 Tablespoons Matcha

1/4 Teaspoon Salt
2 Ripe Avocados
1/2 Teaspoon Lemon Juice
1 1/2 Teaspoons Vanilla Extract

1 7.4-Ounce Can (1 Cup) Sweetened
    Adzuki Beans (Optional)

Matcha can be very tricky to dissolve in any liquid, so it's best to bring out the big guns here. Combine the non-dairy milk, agave, arrowroot, matcha, and salt together in your blender, and purée to incorporate the matcha. Once homogeneous, pour the liquid into a medium saucepan and set over medium heat. Whisk occasionally until the mixture comes up to a full, rolling boil, and then turn off the heat.

Returning to your blender, pit, peel, and toss in the avocados along with the lemon juice and vanilla. Pulse to start breaking down the avocados; then introduce the cooked matcha custard as well. Purée thoroughly, until completely smooth. Let cool before moving into your fridge to chill completely before churning; three hours minimum.

Churn in your ice cream machine according to the manufacturer's instructions. Within the final five minutes of churning, slowly add in the sweetened adzuki beans, if using. Allow the moving paddle to gradually incorporate them into the mixture. Once properly frozen and with adzuki beans evenly distributed throughout, transfer scoops of the soft ice cream into an airtight container. Before serving, store in your freezer for at least three more hours to set up.

Mocha-Maca Rocket Fuel

Makes About
1 Quart

Maca is said to be the secret to increased stamina, frequently utilized by ancient warriors. I can't personally lay claim to any battle victories that maca has guided me to, but all the hype aside, I happen to love that malty, butterscotch flavor, echoing the dark, roasted notes of the coffee so well. Whether it's the caffeine or superfood content at work, this is one powerful snack sure to liven up the afternoon blah doldrums!

2/3 Cup Granulated Sugar
2 Tablespoons Maca Powder
1–2 Tablespoons Instant Coffee
  Powder
2 Tablespoons Cocoa Powder

2 Tablespoons Cornstarch
3 Cups Plain, Non-Dairy Milk
1/4 Cup Light Agave Nectar
1 Teaspoon Vanilla Extract

1/2 Cup Vegan Chocolate-Covered
  Espresso Beans, Roughly
  Chopped

In a medium saucepan, begin by combining the sugar, maca, instant coffee, cocoa powder, and cornstarch. Pour in about 1/3 cup of the non-dairy milk, and whisk thoroughly to create a thick paste with the dry ingredients. Beat vigorously to ensure that there are no clumps of dry goods remaining, taking particular care to scrape the corners of the pan, where there may be pockets of unmixed ingredients lurking. Once smooth, add in the remainder of the non-dairy milk, as well as the agave.

Set on the stove over moderate heat and whisk periodically, until the mixture reaches a full boil. Reduce the heat slightly to maintain a brisk simmer and cook for an additional two minutes. Turn off the heat, whisk in the vanilla, and let cool to room temperature before chilling in the fridge for at least three hours.

Churn in your ice cream machine according to the manufacturer's directions. In the last five minutes of churning, gradually sprinkle in the chopped espresso beans so that the paddle of the machine incorporates and distributes the pieces throughout the ice cream. Transfer the soft ice cream to an airtight container, and store it in the freezer for another three hours minimum, or until frozen solid, before serving.

Purple Cow Ice Cream

Makes About
3 Cups

Conjure up the flavors of that soda shop favorite, typically made with vanilla ice cream and grape soda. In this fun, frozen twist, roles are reversed, and grape ice cream is the star of the show. Serve in a tall glass with cream soda for the full complement of tastes and textures!

1 3/4 Cups Plain, Non-Dairy Milk

3/4 Cup (1/2 of a 12-Ounce Can) Frozen 100% Concord Grape Juice Concentrate, Thawed

Pinch Salt

This is the best ice cream for beginners, as it truly could not be any easier to prepare. Just whisk everything together thoroughly in a medium-sized bowl until homogeneous; then chill for at least thirty minutes. Churn in your ice cream maker according to the manufacturer's instructions and transfer to an airtight container before stashing in the freezer. Let rest in the freezer for at least three hours before serving, until solid enough to scoop.

Root Beer Ice Cream

Makes 1 Quart

Ages ago, when my sister and I were but wee tots and my parents still attempted to restrict our intake of sweets, I remember the harshest restrictions being placed on soda. Needless to say, things have changed quite a bit since then, but my appreciation of root beer remains the same. When it comes to making a root beer float, rather than dilute that luscious brown beverage with some other competing flavor, I much prefer to cut right to the chase and indulge in pure root beer ice cream instead.

1 3/4 Cups Plain, Non-Dairy Milk

1 1/2 Cups Root Beer Soda (NOT Diet)
2/3 Cup Granulated Sugar

2 Tablespoons Arrowroot
1/4 Teaspoon Salt
1 1/2 Tablespoons Root Beer Extract

Whisk together all the ingredients, except for the root beer extract, in a medium saucepan. Beat vigorously to ensure that there are no lumps whatsoever before turning on the heat to medium. Cook, whisking every few minutes, until the mixture comes to a rapid boil; then immediately remove from the stove. Whisk in the root beer extract, and then chill thoroughly before churning according to your ice cream manufacturer's instructions. Transfer the churned ice cream into an airtight container, and stash in the freezer for at least four to six hours before scooping, or until frozen solid.

Shirley Temple Sorbet

Makes 1 Quart

As a kid, before I could begin dreaming of uttering the words to order a Shirley Temple soda, the caveat that "it's a party" had to first be well understood. Always prefacing the drink order with that exact statement, it became ingrained in my head that this was a special drink, not meant for the everyday outing. With time and repetition though, that clause lost its meaning, and any fun outing could be considered a party. Now it takes a bit more consideration to elevate this treat to be worthy of a "party" yet again. A quick spin through the trusty old ice cream machine takes care of that, no sweat.

3 Cups Ginger Ale (NOT Diet)
1/2 Cup Light Corn Syrup
Zest of 1 Lime

Zest of 1 Lemon
1/4 Cup Liquid from Maraschino
　　Cherries, or Grenadine*

1/2 Cup Maraschino Cherries,
　　Chopped

As quickly as you can whisk, you can get this sweet treat churning away. Just mix together everything except for the chopped cherries so that you have a homogeneous liquid. Chill thoroughly if not already cold, and churn in your ice cream maker according to the manufacturer's recommendations.

In the last five minutes of churning, gradually add the chopped maraschino cherries so that the blades of the paddle will incorporate and distribute the pieces throughout the sorbet. Transfer the soft sorbet to an airtight container, and store it in the freezer for six hours minimum, or until frozen solid, before serving.

Garnish with additional maraschino cherries, if desired.

*Grenadine is not an ingredient I typically keep on hand, so my thrifty fix was to use some of the excess liquid that the maraschino cherries are packed in. For a more authentic Shirley Temple, seek out the traditional pomegranate syrup in the soda/mixers section of most grocery stores, or easily make your own at home. To do so, combine equal parts by weight pomegranate juice and granulated sugar. Simmer for fifteen minutes, cool, bottle, and store in the fridge until you're ready to imbibe.

Thai Iced Cream

Makes 1 to 1 1/2 Quarts Thai Ice Cream and 2 Cups Sweetened Condensed Coconut Milk

My first exposure to Thai food yielded the discovery of the elixir known as Thai iced tea. Clear ice cubes bobbed in a tall glass of strong, dark amber tea, carrying the faint whisper of exotic spices I could only venture a guess at. Thick, super-sweet evaporated milk pooled on top, slowly swirling down to the bottom of the glass in enchanting ribbons.

Taking a page from that concept, to fully experience Thai Iced Cream, I must insist upon a generous pour of sweetened condensed coconut milk. Although it is optional, it really ties the whole dessert together. Plus, served warm, it creates an irresistible contrast in temperature that will make this ice cream just as memorable as my first experience with Thai food.

Thai Iced Cream:

2 Cups Plain Vegan Creamer
2 Cups Plain, Non-Dairy Milk
5 Tablespoons Loose Leaf Black Tea
1 Star Anise, Crushed
1/4 Teaspoon Ground Cardamom
Tiny Pinch Ground Cloves
Tiny Pinch Ground Cinnamon

1 Cup Granulated Sugar
2 Tablespoons Arrowroot
1 1/2 Tablespoons Cornstarch
Pinch Salt
2–3 Tablespoons Beet Juice
  (Optional, for Coloring)

1/2 Teaspoon Vanilla Extract
1/4 Teaspoon Orange Blossom Water

Sweetened Condensed Coconut Milk (Optional):

2 Cans Coconut Milk
1/2 Cup Agave Nectar

In a medium saucepan, combine the creamer and non-dairy milk, along with the tea leaves and spices. Bring the mixture up to a full boil before turning off the heat. Cover and let the "milks" steep and infuse for twenty to thirty minutes. Strain out the whole spices and return the smooth liquid to the saucepan once again.

Separately, whisk together the sugar, arrowroot, cornstarch, and salt, mixing well to evenly distribute all of the dry goods. Slowly sift this mixture into the saucepan while whisking briskly. Give it another good whisk through before turning on the heat to medium, to ensure that there are no remaining clumps. Stir periodically, to make sure that the base doesn't scorch, and bring to a vigorous boil. Turn down the heat to medium-low, and simmer for an additional two minutes, at which point the mixture should have thickened quite a bit. Turn off the heat, and incorporate the beet juice if using, vanilla extract, and orange blossom water. Cool and chill in the fridge for at least three hours, until completely cold all the way through.

Churn in your ice cream maker according to the manufacturer's instructions. Transfer to an airtight container, and stash in your freezer for at least three hours before scooping and serving.

For the sweetened condensed coconut milk, simply combine the coconut milk and sugar in a medium saucepan, and bring to a boil. Turn down the heat, allowing it to bubble away at a gentle simmer, until reduced by half. The amount of time required will vary depending on the size and shape of the pan you're using, so keep an eye on it and check in periodically. The best way to measure its progress is by using a wooden dowel or skewer. Dip it into the liquid right at the beginning of the process, and mark the level that it comes up to with a permanent and waterproof marker or pen. When the liquid reaches half that height, it's done! Let cool for at least twenty-five minutes before serving, or chill thoroughly and store in an airtight jar in the fridge for up to two weeks.

Turkish Coffee Ice Cream

Makes About
1 Quart

Making a cup of coffee is a time-honored, complex ritual in Turkey. Brewed in an ornate metal *ibrik* directly over the stove, the ground coffee is heaped straight into the vessel and never filtered. Though it may be a turnoff to some, the grounds are welcome to settle to the bottom in a thick sludge, adding body to the whole drink and supposedly telling the drinker's fortune. Brewed with just a pinch of cardamom for intrigue and prodigious measures of sugar, it's by no means your standard cup of Joe.

3 Cups Plain, Non-Dairy Milk
3/4 Cup Granulated Sugar
2 Tablespoons Arrowroot

3 Tablespoons Instant Coffee Powder
1 Tablespoon Finely Ground Coffee
  Beans

1/4 Teaspoon Ground Cardamom
Pinch Salt

Whisk everything together in a medium saucepan, beating thoroughly and scraping the corners of the pot to ensure that there are no lumps whatsoever before turning on the heat to medium. Cook, whisking every few minutes, until the mixture comes to a rapid boil, and immediately remove from the stove. Chill for at least three hours, until completely cold, before churning according to your ice cream manufacturer's instructions. Transfer into an airtight container, and stash in the freezer for at least three hours before scooping and serving.

White Russian Ice Cream

Makes About
1 Quart

Fine cocktail or alcoholic milkshake? You be the judge. Luckily, the natural dessert-like quality to this mixed drink serves it well as a frozen confection, creating a spiked coffee treat that even "The Dude" might enjoy.

2 Cups Plain, Non-Dairy Milk
1 12-Ounce Package Extra-Firm
   Silken Tofu
2/3 Cup Granulated Sugar
2 Tablespoons Cornstarch

2 Tablespoons Instant Coffee Powder
1/4 Cup Kahlua® or Coffee Liqueur
1 1/2 Teaspoons Vanilla Extract

1/2 Cup Vegan White Chocolate
   Chips or Chopped Homemade
   White Chocolate (page 225)
   (Optional)

In the container of your blender, combine the non-dairy milk, tofu, sugar, cornstarch, and instant coffee. Give it a good blend on high speed until thoroughly puréed. Pause to scrape down the sides of the container as needed, to ensure that everything becomes incorporated and perfectly smooth. Transfer the mixture to a medium saucepan, and set it over moderate heat on the stove. Whisk occasionally until the liquid comes to a rolling boil. Reduce the heat slightly to keep it at a lively simmer, and cook for two minutes longer. Remove the pan from the stove, and stir in the Kahlua and vanilla. Cool to room temperature before refrigerating for at least three hours before proceeding.

Churn in your ice cream machine according to the manufacturer's directions. In the last five minutes of churning, slowly sprinkle in the white chocolate so that the paddle of the machine incorporates and distributes the pieces throughout the ice cream. Transfer the soft ice cream to an airtight container, and store it in the freezer for another three hours minimum, or until frozen solid, before serving.

IN A NUTSHELL: NUTS AND SEEDS

Beurre Noisette Ice Cream

Makes
1–1 1/2 Quarts

Otherwise known as browned butter, the French have a much more elegant way of describing this rich nectar. It is known to the French as "hazelnut butter," alluding to the toasty, hazelnut-like flavor derived from a quick flash in the pan. The application of gentle heat transforms this everyday substance into something otherworldly, redolent with both salty and savory notes that heighten the sweetness of baked goods, or in this case, frozen treats. Many chefs would have you believe that this decadent substance can only be made with dairy, but au contraire! A generous handful of hazelnuts cranks up the volume of that naturally nutty essence, so really, who needs the dairy anyway?

1/2 Cup Non-Dairy Margarine
3 1/4 Cups Plain, Non-Dairy Milk
2 Tablespoons Arrowroot
2/3 Cup Granulated Sugar

1/4 Cup Light Corn Syrup or Light
    Agave Nectar
1/2 Teaspoon Vanilla Extract
1/2 Teaspoon Salt

1/2 Cup Toasted Hazelnuts, Finely
    Chopped

Cut the margarine into tablespoon-sized pieces, and place them in a medium saucepan over medium-low heat. Wait for all of the margarine to melt; then begin swirling the pan around to stir, as needed. In a fairly short time, it should begin to look somewhat separated, with a foamy white top and yellow oil underneath that will gradually progress to a darker color. Eventually, the solids will settle to the bottom and begin to brown. The best judge of doneness here is to watch and listen to the bubbles; they will start making a more hollow pinging sort of sound near the end, and slow nearly to stopping.

At that point, quickly add in the sugar, whisking slowly but continuously. The mixture will be clumpy initially, but it will smooth out. Cook the sugar to a deep amber color, but do not be alarmed if it's still not completely dissolved yet. Add in 1 1/2 cups of the non-dairy milk very carefully to arrest the caramelization process—stand back, because it will sputter angrily. Things may look like a mess now, with the sugar solidified and clumped at the bottom of the pan, but do not panic! Continue stirring over gentle heat until the sugar melts and becomes smooth again.

Whisk the arrowroot and remaining milk together separately before adding them into the pan with the corn syrup and salt. Turn the heat up to medium, bring the mixture to a full boil, and turn off the stove. Stir in the vanilla, and let cool to room temperature before moving the cooked custard into your fridge. Chill thoroughly, for at least three hours, before churning.

Churn in your ice cream machine according to the manufacturer's directions. In the last five minutes of churning, slowly sprinkle in the chopped hazelnuts so that the blades of the paddle incorporate and distribute the nuts throughout the ice cream. Transfer the soft ice cream to an airtight container, and store it in the freezer for at least three hours before serving.

Curried Peanut Butter Ice Cream

Makes 1 Quart

Askillfully crafted curry is all about balance—blending the pungent spices so that no one element overrules the rest, and tempering the inherent heat of chilies and peppers with naturally sweet ingredients. It struck me one evening, while eating this rich and comforting meal, that the balance could just as easily be tipped the other way, into dessert, with a few modifications. While it may sound crazy, consider it another set of spices, like chai or gingerbread, that need just the right supporting team to shine.

1/2 Cup Creamy Peanut Butter
1 Cup Granulated Sugar
1 13.5-Ounce Can (1 3/4 Cups) Full-Fat Coconut Milk

3/4 Cup Plain, Non-Dairy Milk
2–3 Teaspoons Mellow Curry Powder (page 207) or Madras Curry Powder

1/4 Teaspoon Salt
1 1/2 Teaspoons Vanilla Extract

No need to heat up the kitchen at all for this ice cream base! Simply vigorously whisk together all of the ingredients in a large bowl or measuring pitcher until perfectly smooth. You can make this process even easier by tossing everything into your blender instead and giving it a quick blitz. Start with 2 teaspoons of the curry powder, and add more to taste if desired, bearing in mind that the finished ice cream won't be quite as sharp—make it only slightly spicier than you want it to be when it's all done.

Chill the mixture, if not already cold, before churning in your ice cream maker according to the manufacturer's recommendations. Transfer to an airtight container, and let cure in the freezer for at least three hours before serving, to further solidify.

Gianduja Ice Cream

Makes
1–1 1/2 Quarts

Like two adoring lovers, chocolate and hazelnut are nearly inseparable in the pastry kitchen. And considering how beautifully they work together, why struggle to force them apart? Gianduja, the Italian version of this sweet pairing is an excellent example. Some modern confectioners have been known to bend the rules, substituting with almonds or walnuts, but hazelnut is truly irreplaceable in such a classic duo.

1 Cup Toasted Hazelnuts
2 1/2 Cups Plain, Non-Dairy Milk,
　Divided
1 Medium-Sized, Ripe Avocado,
　Pitted

1 Teaspoon Lemon Juice
1 Cup Granulated Sugar
1 Tablespoon Arrowroot
1/2 Teaspoon Salt

3 Ounces (1/2 Cup) Semi-Sweet
　Chocolate Chips
1 Teaspoon Vanilla Extract

Coarsely chop the hazelnuts, and toss them into a medium saucepan along with 1 1/2 cups of the non-dairy milk. Turn on the heat to medium, and cook the mixture just to the brink of boiling. Remove the pan from the stove, cover, and let the hazelnuts infuse the "milk" with their nutty aroma. Allow the mixture to come to room temperature slowly to extract as much flavor from the nuts as possible; wait at least four hours before proceeding.

Move the soaked hazelnuts and "milk" into your blender and add in the avocado flesh and lemon juice as well. Purée on high speed, until thoroughly blended and as smooth as possible. Pause to scrape down the sides of the work bowl periodically, to make sure that there are no large chunks of avocado or hazelnuts that are missing the blade. Allow a full three to six minutes of straight processing for the best texture. Strain the mixture through a fine mesh sieve, and set aside.

Separately, in a medium saucepan, combine the remaining cup of non-dairy milk, sugar, arrowroot, and salt, and set over moderate heat on the stove. Bring it up to a full, rolling boil while whisking periodically; then turn off the heat. Introduce the chocolate and vanilla extract, stirring gently until the chocolate chips melt from the residual heat. Cool, and slowly whisk in the strained hazelnut mixture so that the base is silky and homogeneous. Chill thoroughly in the fridge.

Churn in your ice cream machine according to the manufacturer's instructions, and transfer to an airtight container. Give the ice cream at least three hours in the freezer to harden a bit before serving.

Malted, Salted Cashew Ice Cream

**Makes About
1 Quart**

Regular salted cashews are easy to get hooked on, but that's nothing compared to the addictive power of candied cashews. It's disconcertingly effortless to mindlessly crunch through handfuls of those bite-sized morsels. Re-creating that dangerous taste sensation in ice cream format was just asking for trouble, and precisely as I had feared, I came up with an even more habit-forming treat by adding malt syrup into the mix. Don't say I didn't warn you . . .

2/3 Cup Malted Barley Syrup
1/4 Cup Granulated Sugar
2 3/4 Cup Plain, Non-Dairy Milk

2 Tablespoons Arrowroot
3/4 Cup Salted and Roasted Cashews, Divided

2 Tablespoons Non-Dairy Margarine
1 1/2 Teaspoons Vanilla Extract

Malted barley syrup can be exceedingly sticky, so to make it a bit easier to manage, first lightly grease your measuring cup before dosing out the required amount. It should then slide right out with little difficulty. Pour the malt syrup into the canister of your blender, along with the sugar, non-dairy milk, arrowroot, and 1/4 cup of the cashews. Roughly chop the remainder of the nuts, and set them aside for later.

Blend on high speed until the nuts are completely pulverized and the whole mixture is nice and smooth. Pass through a fine strainer if not using a high-powered blender, to make sure no unpleasant coarse crumbs of the cashews remain. Transfer the smooth base into a medium saucepan, and begin to cook over moderate heat. Whisk periodically until it reaches a rapid bubble. Turn off the heat, and add in the margarine and vanilla. Continue to stir gently until the margarine has all melted and become incorporated. Cool, and then chill for at least three hours.

Churn the cooked custard in your ice cream maker according to the manufacturer's instructions. In the final five minutes of churning, introduce the remaining chopped cashews directly into the blades of the machine, to evenly distribute the pieces throughout the soft ice cream. Transfer to an airtight container, and store in the freezer for at least three hours before serving.

Maple-Pecan Ice Cream

Makes About
1 Quart

Skyrocketing prices mean that access to real maple syrup has become a luxury, so when I do splurge and buy a bottle of the amber nectar, I want to make sure it's prominently featured. This ice cream definitely lets maple steal the show, but you'll still notice the generous helping of toasted pecans singing sweetly in the background. Of course, the best serving suggestion I might offer is to top it with an additional drizzle of maple syrup!

1 1/4 Cups Chopped, Toasted
Pecans, Divided

2 Tablespoons Cornstarch
2 Cups Plain, Non-Dairy Milk

2/3 Cup Grade-B Maple Syrup
1 Tablespoon Amaretto (Optional)

Start by placing 1 cup of the chopped pecans in your food processor or blender, and pulse them until the nuts become a fine flour. Place the pecan meal in a medium saucepan along with the cornstarch and non-dairy milk, and whisk thoroughly to ensure that there are no lumps of starch. Set over medium heat and cook, whisking occasionally, until the mixture just comes to a boil. Turn off the heat, and stir in the maple syrup and amaretto. Cover and let cool for at least thirty minutes.

Move the whole mixture back into your food processor or blender, and give it a good spin, for around four to five minutes, to make sure the nuts are as finely ground as possible. If you're not confident of your appliance, pass the ice cream base through a fine sieve to make sure there's no residual grit or large particles that it may have failed to pulverize.

Chill in the refrigerator for at least one hour before churning in your ice cream maker according to the manufacturer's instructions. In the last five minutes of churning, sprinkle in the remaining 1/4 cup of chopped pecans.

Transfer the soft ice cream into an airtight container, and let rest in the freezer for at least three hours before serving, until solid enough to scoop.

Marzipan Madness Ice Cream

Makes 1 Quart

I thought of calling this recipe "Marzipan Supernova Ice Cream," but due to the negative connotations of violently exploding food, I thought better of it. However, the point is that no matter what you call it, this ice cream is a multidimensional almond experience. The humble nut could have only dreamed of such glory, being incorporated via sliced almonds, marzipan, and almond extract. If you go all out and select almond milk as your non-dairy milk of choice, you could create a full-fledged quadruple almond ice cream, too!

1 7-Ounce Tube Marzipan, Roughly
    Chopped
2 Cups Plain, Non-Dairy Milk
2/3 Cup Granulated Sugar

2 Tablespoons Maple Syrup
1 1/2 Tablespoons Arrowroot
1/4 Teaspoon Salt
Pinch Ground Nutmeg

1/2 Teaspoon Almond Extract
1/2 Teaspoon Vanilla Extract
1/2 Cup Toasted, Sliced Almonds

Place the marzipan pieces and half of the non-dairy milk in a medium saucepan over medium-low heat on the stove. Cook gently for five to eight minutes, stirring frequently, until the marzipan dissolves into the mixture. Separately, mix together the remaining "milk," sugar, maple syrup, arrowroot, salt, and nutmeg. Stir vigorously to break up any lumps before adding it into the saucepan.

Turn up the heat slightly to medium and continue to whisk gently. Bring the mixture up to a rapid boil; then immediately turn off the heat. Add in both extracts, stir to combine, and let cool. Chill thoroughly for at least three hours before churning according to your ice cream manufacturer's instructions. In the last five minutes of churning, pour the sliced almonds right into the machine, allowing the paddle to incorporate the nuts into the soft ice cream as it continues to turn.

Transfer into an airtight container, and let the ice cream harden a bit in the freezer, at least three hours, before serving.

Peanut Butter Bombshell Ice Cream

Makes
1–1 1/2 Quarts

When it comes to peanut butter, there's just no middle ground—either you love or loathe that sticky paste. I personally can't get enough of it, especially when it comes to dessert. Packed with nutty goodness all around, this rich frozen delight is loaded up with creamy peanut butter, chopped peanuts, and peanut butter-filled sandwich cookies. File this one under "peanut butter lovers only!"

1 Cup Creamy Peanut Butter
1/3 Cup Granulated Sugar
1/3 Cup Dark Brown Sugar, Firmly
  Packed

2 Cups Plain, Non-Dairy Milk
1 Tablespoon Cornstarch
1/2 Teaspoon Salt
1 Teaspoon Vanilla Extract

1/2 Cup Roughly Chopped Roasted
  Peanuts
10 Peanut Butter-Filled Chocolate
  Sandwich Cookies*

In a medium saucepan, vigorously whisk together the peanut butter, both of the sugars, non-dairy milk, cornstarch, and salt. Make sure that there are no lumps remaining, and place on the stove over medium heat. Whisk frequently but gently, taking care to scrape the bottom and sides of the pan while the base comes up to temperature. Cook until bubbles begin to break on the surface and the liquid seems significantly thickened. Remove from the heat, and whisk in the vanilla. Let cool before moving the mixture into the fridge. Chill thoroughly, or for at least three hours, before churning in your ice cream maker according to the manufacturer's instructions.

While it churns, chop the sandwich cookies into quarters. In the last five minutes of churning, add in the peanuts and cookies.

Transfer the soft ice cream into an airtight container, and let rest in the freezer for at least three hours before serving, until solid enough to scoop.

> Not as wild about the little goobers as I am? Any other nut butter (such as cashew, almond, or even macadamia) would make a fine replacement.

> To satisfy a salty snack craving, try substituting crushed dark chocolate-covered pretzels OR peanut butter-filled pretzel nuggets for the cookies!

*Can't find this specialty snack? Not to worry, the standard vanilla crème-filled cookies will be perfectly delicious as well.

Although the cookies may seem superfluous in this ultra-rich base, don't be tempted to omit them altogether. That little hit of chocolate and crunchy texture really adds a ton of depth to this otherwise one-note ice cream. If need be, you could add in 4 ounces of finely chopped semi-sweet chocolate instead.

Pistachio Praline Ice Cream

Makes 1 - 1 1/2 Quarts Pistachio Ice Cream / About 2 Cups Pistachio Praline Paste

Every pistachio ice cream I've met has had an identity crisis. Though it may call itself pistachio and shine with an otherworldly hue of green, the main flavor is actually coming from almond extract.

My rendition cuts no corners and doesn't skimp on the pistachios. Emphasizing their natural flavor, the toasted and caramelized flavors are brought to the party by first creating a praline paste to make it even more full-bodied.

Pistachio Ice Cream Base:

1 Cup Pistachio Praline Paste*
1 1/2 Cups Raw Baby Spinach, Packed
1 Medium-Sized, Ripe Avocado, Pitted
1 Teaspoon Lemon Juice

2 1/4 Cups Plain, Non-Dairy Milk
1 Cup Granulated Sugar
1 Teaspoon Vanilla Extract
1/4 Teaspoon Salt

Pistachio Praline Paste:

1 Cup Granulated Sugar
1/4 Cup Water
2 Cups Shelled, Skinned and Toasted Pistachios
3/4 Teaspoon Salt
1 Tablespoon Olive Oil

First, make the pistachio praline paste. Place the sugar and water in a medium saucepan over moderate heat. Stir to combine and bring to a boil. Allow the sugar to cook until it caramelizes to a deep amber color, about ten to fifteen minutes. Quickly add in the pistachios, stir to coat with the hot sugar, and immediately transfer everything out to a silpat or piece of parchment paper. Let cool completely before breaking it into chunks, and tossing the pieces into your food processor, along with the salt and oil. Pulse to break down the brittle to a coarse consistency, and then let the motor run until very smooth. It may take as long as ten minutes, so be patient. Let cool before using, or store in an airtight container in the fridge for up to two weeks.

For the cleanest pistachio flavor and richest emerald-green color, seek out pistachios from Sicily. Even if it's made with any old pistachios, this version is a world apart from those almond imposters.

For the ice cream base, toss first four ingredients into your blender in precisely the order called for. Start the machine on a low setting, just to get everything moving and the spinach leaves incorporated and broken down a bit so that they don't take up quite so much space. Add in the remaining components, starting the blender slowly again, but gradually cranking up the pace until it's at a full purée.

Blend very thoroughly, until the sugar is dissolved and the spinach seems to disappear into a pleasantly green glow throughout the mixture; there should be no remaining flecks of whole leaves. If using a standard blender, this will take a bit more time, and a careful straining through a fine mesh sieve afterwards. Regardless, try to blend only as much as necessary to prevent the machine from overheating, "cooking" the spinach, and turning it brown.

Transfer the base to a cool container, and chill in the fridge for at least three hours before proceeding.

Churn in your ice cream maker according to the manufacturer's instructions. Scoop the soft ice cream into an air-tight container, and stash it in your freezer for at least three hours before serving.

*If the idea of making the praline paste is intimidating, forget I ever mentioned it; there's no shame in using jarred pistachio butter instead. It will lack the complexity of the praline, but still have a luscious pistachio flavor all its own. If you can get past the initial sticker shock, any pistachio butter that contains only nuts, perhaps a bit of salt, and maybe a tiny bit of sugar will work beautifully.

Pup-sicles

Makes 8 – 12
Treats, Depending
on the Size and
Shape of Your
Molds

When it comes time for dessert, don't forget about your four-legged friends! Though my pup, Isis, would probably be happy enough just to crunch away on ice cubes, she's much more eager to snatch up these nutritious frozen biscuits when offered. They're perfectly edible for creatures of the two-legged variety as well, but bear in mind that they're not particularly sweet, so I might suggest adding a tablespoon of maple syrup or agave if you wanted one for yourself.

1/4 Cup Crunchy, Unsalted Peanut
    Butter
1 Tablespoon Unsulfured Molasses

1/2 Cup Plain, Unsweetened Soy
    Yogurt

1 Tablespoon Flax Seeds, Ground
    (Optional)

    Simply whisk together all of the ingredients until smooth, and then pour the mixture into popsicle or ice cube molds of any shape desired. For a traditional bone shape, you can find molds either online or in some specialty cooking and baking stores. Just remember to select smaller one- or two-bite shapes so that the treats don't melt all over your carpet while your furry friend savors his or her dessert. Do not add sticks to popsicles for puppies, as they can become choking hazards.

Rosemary-Pecan Ice Cream

Makes
1–1 1/2 Quarts

As a back-up holiday gift to friends and family who claim to lack a true sweet tooth, punchy spiced pecans appeal to all palates. Inspired by that runaway success, I figured that the same universal approval would follow if I could convert that combination to an ice cream flavor. Rosemary, though perhaps unexpected, is a key element that brings this bold ice cream flavor together, adding a welcome, vibrant herbal note at the finish.

1 1/4 Cups Toasted Pecan Halves, Chopped and Divided
1 Tablespoon Non-Dairy Margarine
1/3 Cup Grade-B Maple Syrup

2/3 Cup Dark Brown Sugar, Firmly Packed
3/4 Teaspoon Ground Cinnamon
1/4–1/2 Teaspoon Cayenne Pepper
1/2 Teaspoon Salt

1 Tablespoon Fresh or 1 Teaspoon Dried Rosemary, Chopped
3 Tablespoons Cornstarch
2 1/2 Cups Plain, Non-Dairy Milk

Set aside 1/4 cup of the chopped pecans for later; then place the rest in a medium saucepan, along with the margarine. Cook over medium heat until aromatic.

Meanwhile, whisk together the remaining ingredients in a separate container. When the whole kitchen begins to smell nutty and toasty, pour in the liquid mixture and stir well to incorporate.

Cook, stirring often, until the mixture comes up to a rapid boil. Turn down the heat slightly so that it doesn't bubble over, and continue to stir for another two minutes. Remove the pan from the heat.

Carefully pour the hot base into your blender, and gradually crank the machine up to full power. Purée thoroughly, until the nuts are completely broken down and smooth. If you don't have a high-speed blender, give it at least eight to ten minutes. The mixture may still be slightly gritty even when it looks silky-smooth, so pass it through a fine mesh sieve lined with cheesecloth to catch any remaining pecan particles.

Cool to room temperature; then chill thoroughly in your fridge.

Give the base at least three hours to sit; then churn in your ice cream maker according to the manufacturer's instructions. In the final five minutes of churning, add the remaining chopped pecans right into the mix, allowing the paddle to stir the pieces in for you. Scoop the soft ice cream into an airtight container, and let rest in the freezer for at least three hours to further solidify before serving.

Salt and Pepper Sunflower Seed Ice Cream

**Makes About
1 Quart**

Salt and pepper ice cream? Though not a flavor most people would consider, I was still convinced that there was enormous potential in that quirky concept, even after an initially disastrous kitchen experiment. I just couldn't let the idea go. By using nutty sunflower seed butter as a subtle backdrop, it's almost like bringing in a referee to help mediate a feuding couple. They really can get along, quite harmoniously in fact, with one more friend to help bring out their best qualities.

2 3/4 Cups Plain, Non-Dairy Milk
1/2 Cup Sunflower Seed Butter
3/4 Cup Light Agave Nectar
1 1/2 Tablespoons Arrowroot

1/4–1/2 Teaspoon Ground Black
   Pepper
1 1/2 Teaspoons Vanilla Extract

1/2 Cup Roasted and Salted, Shelled
   Sunflower Seeds

Whisk together all of the ingredients, except for the whole sunflower seeds, in a large bowl or measuring pitcher until perfectly smooth. You can make this process even easier by tossing the components into your blender instead and giving it a quick blitz.

Chill the mixture if not already cold, before churning in your ice cream maker according to the manufacturer's recommendations. In the last five minutes of churning, sprinkle the sunflower seeds right into the machine, letting the paddle distribute the seeds throughout the soft ice cream as it continues to spin. Transfer to an airtight container, and let cure in the freezer for at least three hours before serving, to further solidify.

NATURE'S CANDY:

FRUITS, VEGETÁBLES, AND HERBS

Banana Split Ice Cream

Makes 1–1 1/2
Quarts

Towering scoops of vanilla ice cream nestled between two halves of a sliced banana, topped with a river of hot fudge sauce and buried under an avalanche of all manner of crunchy chopped nuts and sprinkles, the quintessential banana split is all about excess. Scoop out an instant sundae every time, and save yourself the headache of keeping all the fresh ingredients at their prime for just one or two celebratory sundaes. Top the whole thing off with a fresh cherry, and every day can be a sundae.

1 1/2 Pounds (4–5 Large) Peeled, Ripe Bananas
1/2 Cup Granulated Sugar
2 Tablespoons Light Corn Syrup or Light Agave Nectar
1 Cup Full-Fat Coconut Milk

1/2 Cup Fresh or Frozen and Thawed Strawberries, Chopped
1/4 Cup Roasted Peanuts or Walnuts, Chopped

1/2 Cup (3 Ounces) Semi-Sweet Chocolate Chips
1/2 Teaspoon Canola Oil

This is a very simple base where the freshest, best ingredients are what truly sets it apart, so don't skimp! Just toss the ripe bananas into your food processor along with the sugar, corn syrup, and coconut milk, and purée until completely smooth. Pause to scrape down the interior of the blender as needed to ensure that there are no chunks of banana left behind. Pass through a fine mesh strainer to filter out any possibly remaining chunks; then chill the thick, pudding-like base in the fridge for at least two hours, until ice-cold.

Churn in your ice cream machine according to the manufacturer's instructions, and while it spins, prep the mix-in components. Have the strawberries and nuts at the ready, and in a separate, microwave-safe dish, combine the chocolate and oil. Microwave at thirty-second intervals, stirring thoroughly after each heating, until completely melted and smooth.

In the final five minutes of churning, slowly add in the berries and nuts, allowing the paddle to incorporate them into the soft ice cream as it continues spinning. Transfer spoonfuls into an airtight container, and drizzle each addition with a very fine ribbon of the liquid chocolate. The chocolate will set up almost immediately upon contact. Once all of the ice cream and chocolate is safely within the container, give the whole mixture a good stir with a wide spatula, breaking up the chocolate ribbon into a fine stracciatella, and distributing all of the mix-ins evenly throughout. Stash in your freezer and let firm up for at least three hours before serving.

Beet Marmalade Ice Cream

Makes About 1
Quart

If there was one recipe to convert any beet-hater, it would have to be this one. I, too, despised the red roots, until I began working at Health in a Hurry, a cozy little vegetarian restaurant in my hometown. One of the signature dishes was the beet marmalade wrap: Onions slowly cooked down to a soft, silken texture and caramelized with maple syrup and orange juice were blended with roasted beets, creating a captivating contrast between sweet and savory. Orange and beet, a seemingly odd couple from afar, actually work in brilliant harmony precisely because they're so different. It may sound like a stretch, but take a leap of faith with this concept; I promise you'll be happily surprised.

1 Cup Plain, Non-Dairy Milk
2 Tablespoons Cornstarch
1 Cup Full-Fat Coconut Milk
2/3 Cup Granulated Sugar

1/4 Cup Grade-B Maple Syrup
1/4 Teaspoon Salt
1 Cup Chopped and Roasted Red
    Beets,* Puréed (About 6 Ounces)

1/2 Cup Orange Juice
Zest of 1/2 Orange
2 Tablespoons Grand Marnier or
    Orange Liqueur (Optional)

Whisk the non-dairy milk and cornstarch together vigorously to create a thin slurry; then pour it into a medium-sized saucepan along with the coconut milk, sugar, maple syrup, and salt. Set the mixture over medium heat, whisking gently until it comes to a full boil. Immediately turn off the heat and whisk in the beet purée, orange juice, orange zest, and orange liqueur if using. Stir until smooth, and then cool to room temperature. Move the base into the fridge to chill thoroughly, for at least three hours, before proceeding.

Churn in your ice cream maker according to the manufacturer's recommendations, and then transfer into an airtight container. Stash in your freezer for at least four hours before serving so that it can further solidify into a scoopable texture.

*Cut out the mess by leaving the skin on the beets prior to roasting. Choose smaller roots to make the process move faster, and wrap them all up in a foil package. Bake at 425 degrees for about an hour, until fork-tender. Let the beets sit until cool enough to handle, and then the skins should just rub off with gentle pressure. If they're still too stubbornly adhered to be removed by hand, a peeler will make quick work of them instead.

Bitter Orange Sorbet

Makes 1 Scant
Quart

One of my earliest memories of any frozen dessert comes from Thanksgiving, circa the early 1990s—orange sorbet. Not just any old wan, oversweetened grocery store orange sorbet, but a strong, bitter, and powerful rendition, made by my grandfather tableside with the oranges he grew himself. As the final bites of dinner lingered on nearly clean plates, everyone would be reaching their limits but unable to refuse such a lavish feast. Though I never was able to get the exact recipe for that bitter orange sorbet from my grandpa, hopefully this comes close enough to do him proud.

Peel of 1 Orange
1 Cup Water
3/4 Cup Granulated Sugar

1 1/4 Cups Fresh Orange Juice*
(4–5 Large Oranges)

1/4 Cup Fresh Grapefruit Juice
1/4 Cup Fresh Lemon Juice

Carefully slice the peel off the whole orange in large strips, removing any of the bitter white pith on the inside by scraping lightly with a paring knife. Place the peel, water, and sugar in a medium saucepan, and bring to a simmer over medium heat. Stir periodically, until the sugar has completely dissolved, about five minutes. Remove the pan from the stove, and cool completely.

Once at room temperature, strain out the orange peel and combine the zesty syrup with the orange juice, grapefruit juice, and lemon juice. Move the sorbet base into the fridge, and chill thoroughly before churning.

Churn in your ice cream maker according to the manufacturer's instructions. Either serve immediately, as a very soft-textured sorbet like my grandpa made, or transfer to an airtight container, and allow at least three hours for it to further solidify in the freezer before serving.

*If you can possibly get your hands on Seville oranges, which are naturally more bitter than the standard juicing or eating varieties, you can substitute their juice for all of the other citrus (1 1/2 cups plus 2 tablespoons total). Just bear in mind that these oranges are very small, so you may need to squeeze as many as twelve to fourteen to yield enough juice.

Black Raspberry Blitz Ice Cream

Makes 1 Quart

Blackberries can come as a tart surprise to someone accustomed only to mild raspberries. That knowledge wasn't enough to stop us crazy urban foragers from harvesting buckets full of those glistening black jewels. Sour and astringent on their own, the magic happens not when eating them raw, but as soon as they become an ice cream ingredient. Those local berries might get passed over by most casual pickers, but with a transformative recipe like this simple dessert, anyone who ignores such a treasure is missing out.

1 Cup (6 Ounces) Blackberries, Fresh or Frozen and Thawed
2 1/2 Cups Plain, Non-Dairy Milk
1/2 Cup Granulated Sugar
1/2 Cup Seedless Raspberry Jam
1 Tablespoon Cornstarch
1/2 Cup Blackberry Jam

Begin by tossing all of the berries, non-dairy milk, sugar, jam, and cornstarch into your blender and puréeing on high speed. Blend until the mixture is as smooth as possible; then strain through a fine mesh sieve to remove any seeds; discard the solids.

Pour the liquid into a medium saucepan, and set over medium heat on the stove. Whisk periodically as it comes up to heat, and bring to a boil. Cook for two additional minutes, stirring constantly, to allow the base to reach its full thickening potential; then immediately turn off the heat to prevent it from bubbling over. Cool, and chill in the fridge for at least three hours.

Churn in your ice cream maker according to the manufacturer's suggestions. Once finished spinning, scoop out about one-third of the still-soft ice cream into an airtight container and drizzle randomly with a third of the blackberry jam. If the jam is too thick to pour, microwave it for a few seconds to loosen it up, but be careful not to get it so hot that it will instantly melt the ice cream. Cover with another one-third of the ice cream, drizzle with more jam, and repeat one final time with the rest. Use a wide spatula to lightly marble the jam all throughout, and quickly move the whole container into the freezer. Let rest for at least four hours to further solidify before serving.

Blood Orange Frozen Yogurt

Makes About
1 Quart

Bold and tangy, the citrus sings in pitch-perfect harmony with the yogurt base. Crunchy shards of caramelized peel add bursts of intense orange flavor, accompanied by deep, burnt sugar notes to round it all out. This recipe takes a bit more patience than your standard frozen dessert, but it is absolutely worth the wait. Blood oranges lend an irresistible crimson hue and an intense but delicately nuanced citrus flavor to this creamy concoction.

3 Cups (1 24-Ounce Container) Plain
  Vegan "Yogurt"
2 Blood Oranges

1/2 Cup Granulated Sugar
1/2 Cup Water
3/4 Cup Light Agave Nectar

2 Tablespoons Grand Marnier,
  Limoncello, or Vodka
1/2 Teaspoon Vanilla Extract

First things first, line a strainer with two layers of cheesecloth, place over a large bowl to catch the drips, and pour in all of the yogurt. Cover the top with another sheet of cheesecloth, and place the plastic yogurt container lid on top of that. Use a can of beans or tomatoes (anything you've got) as a weight by putting it squarely on top of the plastic lid. The lid is there to disperse the weight a bit, and prevent yogurt from squeezing out around the sides of the can. Let sit in a cool place (but not the fridge) for approximately forty-eight hours, until 1/2 cup of "whey" has drained out.

> Regular old oranges can suffice in a pinch, although it won't have quite the same depth and brightness as the original recipe.

Meanwhile, take your oranges and remove the peel in long, thin strips. Cut away as much pith as possible, and reserve the oranges' flesh for later. Place the peels in a small saucepan, and add water to cover. Bring it to a boil, turn off the heat, and thoroughly drain away the liquid. Cover again with fresh water, and repeat this process for a total of three times. This will help to remove excess bitterness.

Next, add in the sugar and 1/2 cup of water, turn on the heat to medium, and bring it to a boil. Once the sugar has dissolved, reduce the heat slightly so that it stays at a gentle simmer. Swirl the pan every few minutes, until the sugar begins to take on a golden amber color. Once the mixture is fully golden brown and caramelized, quickly pour everything out on a silpat or piece of parchment paper, and do your best to separate the peels. Let cool completely before breaking into small shards. Save them in an airtight container to prevent the sugar from melting or softening.

With both of the most difficult elements ready to go, transfer the drained yogurt into your blender or food processor, along with the agave, alcohol of choice, and vanilla. Trim away any remaining white pith from the reserved orange flesh, remove seeds if you spot any, and toss the whole oranges in as well. Blend thoroughly, stopping to scrape down the sides of the bowl as needed, until completely combined and perfectly smooth. Be patient, and don't worry if the mixture becomes rather warm in the process.

Chill thoroughly for at least two hours before churning in your ice cream maker according to the manufacturer's instructions. As you transfer the soft, fresh frozen yogurt into an airtight container, fold in your caramelized orange peel shards. Stash the containers in your freezer for at least four hours before scooping and serving. The peels will soften over time, so this is best served within a week, though it can certainly be stored longer.

Blueberry-Balsamic Ice Cream

Makes 1 Quart

One of those sneaky little tricks for subtly enhancing most any dish is one taught to me by studying ancient Italian cookbooks—a tiny splash of vinegar, particularly balsamic, is the secret to making berries "pop," dazzling with their own inherent flavor. For an even more "authentic" herbal pairing, try switching out the mint for fresh basil.

1 1/2 Cups Blueberries, Fresh or
   Frozen and Thawed
2 Tablespoons Balsamic Vinegar

1/2 Cup Granulated Sugar
1/4 Cup Maple Syrup
2 Cups Plain, Non-Dairy Milk

1 1/2 Tablespoons Arrowroot
1 Tablespoon Fresh Mint Leaves,
   Finely Minced

This ice cream base begins much the same as the procedure for making freezer jam. Place the blueberries, vinegar, sugar, and maple syrup in a medium saucepan, and set over medium-low heat. Cook until the berries burst and stew happily in their own juices for ten to fifteen minutes.

Separately, vigorously beat the arrowroot and non-dairy milk into a loose slurry, double-checking that there are no remaining lumps of starch before pouring the mixture into the pot of stewed berries. Stir well to incorporate, and turn up the heat to medium. Stir periodically until the mixture comes up to a boil; then turn off the heat.

Stir in the fresh mint, cover the pot with the lid, and let sit undisturbed until it cools to room temperature, allowing the mint to infuse. Transfer the whole mixture to your blender and thoroughly purée. Pass through a strainer to ensure the smoothest texture and discard the solids.

Chill in the fridge for at least three hours before churning in your ice cream machine according to the manufacturer's instructions. Scoop the soft ice cream into an airtight container, and let it further solidify in your freezer for at least three hours before serving.

Candied, Brandied Yam Ice Cream

Makes About
1 Quart

One cardinal, unforgivable sin of Thanksgiving food prep is adding marshmallows to sweet potatoes or yams destined for the main meal. Likewise, while yams drenched in brown sugar and brandy are a must for any fall feast worth its salt, they too make much more sense as a sweet finale, not a side dish.

Put them right back with their place in this ice cream. Even Aunt Gertrude, who insists upon serving the jellied canned cranberry sauce that wiggles freely, untouched throughout the whole meal, will be happy to adopt this particular tradition.

1 Pound Yams or Sweet Potatoes, Peeled (About 2–3 Medium Potatoes, or 3 Cups Cubed)
3 Tablespoons Non-Dairy Margarine
2/3 Cup Dark Brown Sugar, Firmly Packed
1/3 Cup Brandy*
1/4 Teaspoon Salt
1/8 Teaspoon Ground Nutmeg
2 1/2 Cups Non-Dairy Milk, Divided

Peel and chop the sweet potatoes into 2-inch chunks. Boil them in a large pot of water for about ten to fifteen minutes, or until fork-tender. Drain and set aside.

In a large skillet set over medium heat, melt the margarine. Stir in the brown sugar, brandy, salt, and 1/4 cup of the "milk," stirring until smooth. Add the sweet potatoes, tossing to coat. Reduce the heat to low, stirring gently at least every ten minutes or so, for thirty minutes until most of the liquid has evaporated and what remains has cooked down to a syrupy consistency.

Turn off the heat, let cool for at least fifteen minutes; then move the candied sweet potatoes into your blender. Follow that with the remaining non-dairy milk and nutmeg, and purée well so that the mixture is perfectly smooth. Chill completely before churning in your ice cream maker according to the manufacturer's instructions. Store the ice cream in an airtight container, and let it rest in your freezer for at least three additional hours before serving.

*If your spirits cabinet is limited, don't feel that you have to run out and splurge on top-shelf brandy to make this recipe. Any sort of rum, bourbon, or, if you're in a more fruity mood, orange liqueur, can fill the bill nicely.

Citrus Zinger Ice Cream

Makes 1 Scant
Quart

Atruly piquant treat for the taste buds, this sophisticated flavor pairing adds up to far more than your average citrus affair. Lemon and orange zests join forces to produce a tantalizingly tart base, accentuated by the unique spiciness of both fresh ginger and black pepper. Bright and funky fresh, it's one quick fix I always turn to when I need a boost fighting off the winter blahs.

1 14-Ounce Can (1 3/4 Cups) Full-
   Fat Coconut Milk
1/2 Cup Plain, Non-Dairy Milk
2/3 Cup Granulated Sugar
1 Teaspoon Arrowroot

1 Tablespoon Cornstarch
2 Tablespoons Orange Zest
1 Tablespoon Lemon Zest
1 Tablespoon Finely Grated Fresh
   Ginger

1/8–1/4 Teaspoon Freshly Ground
   Black Pepper
Pinch Salt
1/2 Teaspoon Vanilla Extract

   Standard, straightforward custard procedure here: vigorously whisk everything together, except for the vanilla, in a medium saucepan, being sure to beat out any lumps of starch before turning on the heat. Dial up the stove to medium heat and whisk occasionally until the mixture comes to a full boil. Stir continuously, and cook for another minute before immediately moving off the heat. Cool, whisk in the vanilla, and then chill in the fridge for at least three hours.

   Once completely cold, churn the cooked custard base in your ice cream maker according to the manufacturer's instructions. Transfer the soft ice cream to an airtight container, and let it rest in your freezer for at least three additional hours before serving.

Cucumber-Melon Sorbet

Makes About
1 Quart

Capable of making anything seem more refreshing than pure water itself, cucumbers deserve further consideration when it comes to keeping cool in the summer. Cucumbers and melons are in fact part of the same botanical family known as "cucurbits," so it's not so far-fetched to bring them together for dessert.

1/2 Pound Watermelon (About 1 1/2 Cups Cubed) or 1 Cup Watermelon Juice (see page 156 for Juicy Watermelon Sorbet)
1/2 Pound Honeydew Melon, Seeded (About 1 1/2 Cups Cubed)

1/2 Pound Cucumber (About 1 1/2 Cups Chopped)
1 Cup Granulated Sugar
Pinch Salt
4–5 Fresh Mint Leaves (Optional)

1 Tablespoon Limoncello or Vodka (Optional)
1/2 Teaspoon Matcha Powder (Optional, For Color)

Go ahead and toss everything into your blender; then purée until all of the fruits are broken down to a smooth consistency and the sugar has dissolved. If your blender can't accommodate such volume all at once, blend in batches with approximately equal amounts of each ingredient. Mix everything together thoroughly; then pass through a fine strainer. Discard the solids and then chill the liquid well.

After at least two hours in the fridge, churn the sorbet base in your ice cream machine according to the manufacturer's directions. Transfer to an airtight container, and stash in your freezer for at least three hours before scooping and serving.

Fresh Corn Ice Cream

Makes About
1 Quart

At the height of summer, when the farmers markets overflow with a rainbow of produce, it's often the most ordinary of edibles that shine the brightest. Corn is just one of these unassuming diamonds in the rough, cursed with easy availability throughout the year in canned and frozen form, and thus not as celebrated as the illustrious heirloom tomatoes, or fleeting and fragile berries, as highly sought after as they are finicky to produce. Corn gets the short end of the stick, because while it's firmly rooted in the vegetable family, it can be as sweet as candy when in its prime.

Yes, corn for dessert! Long since valued for its sweeter properties in many Asian cultures, it's a strange thought to introduce the golden kernels to a silky ice cream base at all. The key here is to only purchase corn on the cob, nothing preserved or pre-shucked, and to reserve this particular recipe only for prime corn season, around July and August. Follow these simple rules, and the natural sugars of the corn will carry your ice cream far, and I promise that corn for dessert won't seem so odd anymore.

3 Ears Fresh, Impeccably Ripe Corn, Shucked (1 1/2–2 Cups Kernels)
2 Tablespoons Non-Dairy Margarine or Coconut Oil
1/4 Cup Granulated Sugar
1/4 Teaspoon Salt
Pinch Freshly Ground Black Pepper
1 Cup Full-Fat Coconut Milk
1 1/2 Cups Plain Non-Dairy Milk
1/2 Cup Agave Nectar
1 1/2 Tablespoons Arrowroot Powder
1/4 Teaspoon Vanilla Extract

Slice the kernels off your cobs of corn, and then run the back of your knife along the cobs to extract as much of the milky liquid as possible. Catch it in a separate bowl and set aside for later.

In a medium saucepan set over medium heat, melt the margarine or coconut oil, and sautée the corn kernels, sugar, salt, and pepper together for about 10 minutes, until lightly caramelized.

Meanwhile, whisk together the coconut milk, non-dairy milk, agave, and arrowroot in a separate bowl, beating vigorously to ensure that there are no lumps of starch remaining. Pour this liquid mixture into the saucepan, whisking thoroughly to incorporate. Bring to a rapid boil and immediately turn off the heat. Let cool for at least 10 minutes before transferring to a blender, and puréeing completely. Pass through a fine mesh strainer if necessary. Place the corn custard in the fridge to thoroughly chill before churning, at least 3 hours.

Once properly chilled, churn in your ice cream maker according to the manufacturer's instructions. Transfer the soft ice cream to an airtight container, and let it rest in your freezer for at least three additional hours before serving.

Grapefruit Mojito Ice Cream

Makes 1 Quart

It was an invention born of desperation. Snowed in with no hope of escaping to a warmer climate, there was little to do and even less to lift our spirits. After going on a light cleaning spree to help pass the time, we remembered the liquor cabinet. While we had no limes, the fridge was bursting with ruby red winter grapefruits. A splash of mint extract made due at the time, but fresh mint really does enhance the drink like nothing else. Now I can't imagine a mojito made any other way.

2 Cups Plain, Non-Dairy Milk
3/4 Cup Granulated Sugar
1 Cup Fresh Mint Leaves, Loosely
    Packed (About 1 Ounce)

Zest of 1/2 Grapefruit (About 1–2
    Tablespoons)
1 Cup Grapefruit Juice

1 Tablespoon Arrowroot
3 Tablespoons Light Rum

Large amounts of citrus or other acidic liquids can often curdle non-dairy milk, so it's best to keep the two separate for as long as possible. Begin with the non-dairy milk and sugar in a medium saucepan over moderate heat. Lightly chop and bruise the mint to release some of the essential oils; then stir the leaves in as well. Bring to the brink of boiling, kill the heat, and cover with the lid. Let steep for thirty minutes before straining out and discarding the spent mint leaves.

Meanwhile, in a separate pot, whisk together the grapefruit zest, juice, and arrowroot, beating vigorously to break up any potential lumps. Turn on the heat to medium, and cook, stirring frequently, until the mixture thickens and comes up to a full boil. Remove the pot from the stove and stir in the rum.

Chill both liquids in their respective containers, until ice-cold, about three hours. Right before churning, combine and thoroughly whisk the two together. Immediately begin to churn in your ice cream machine according to the manufacturer's instructions, and then transfer to an airtight container. Store in your freezer for at least three hours for the mixture to firm up and reach a scoopable consistency.

Jam Ice Cream

Makes 1 Scant
Quart

In a jam and need to whip up some ice cream right away? Well, just reach into the pantry and pull out a trusty jar of—what else?—jam! Consider this a "choose your own adventure" sort of recipe because any jam you have, from grape to blueberry to pineapple, will churn like a dream. Perfect for times when fresh fruits may not be available, this is one super simple formula to ensure that you'll never be without delicious ice cream, no matter the season.

1 Cup Jam (With Sugar and Pectin)   2 Teaspoons Fresh Lemon Juice
1 1/2 Cups Vanilla Non-Dairy Milk

In a medium saucepan, combine all of the ingredients, and whisk gently over medium heat. Cook just until the jam dissolves and your mixture is completely smooth.

Chill for at least one hour in the refrigerator before churning in your ice cream maker according to the manufacturer's instructions.

Transfer the soft ice cream into an airtight container, and let rest in the freezer for at least three hours before serving, until solid enough to scoop.

Can't find any interesting flavors of jam to play with? Try combining different flavors, such as strawberry and plum, or orange marmalade and blueberry. If you want to get real fancy, you could even make your own jam from scratch!

Sugar-free varieties are the only type to be avoided here, so get creative and try giving an interesting new jam a spin.

Juicy Watermelon Sorbet

Makes 1 Quart

Few things are more disappointing than cracking open a lackluster melon, but should you find yourself with one that merely lacks a crisp texture, there's a happy solution. Turn that squishy flesh into refreshing juice instead! Although I often prefer to keep things simple and let the pure essence of watermelon shine, chocolate chips or cocoa nibs do imitate the appearance of seeds remarkably well, which makes for a whimsical presentation.

3 Cups Watermelon Juice*
3/4 Cup Light Agave Nectar
Pinch Salt

1/4 Cup Cacao Nibs or Miniature
   Vegan Chocolate Chips (Optional)

Once you've secured your juice, the rest is child's play. Stir together the juice, agave, and salt, and chill if not already cold. Churn in your ice cream maker according to the manufacturer's recommendations, and if using, sprinkle the nibs or chips into the path of the paddle within the final five minutes of churning. Transfer scoops of the soft sorbet to an airtight container. Let rest in the freezer for at least four hours to further solidify before serving.

*Although I for one would buy it in gallons, pure watermelon juice is sadly unavailable for purchase. The fact that you can't even get the stuff online should speak volumes for its rarity. Luckily, it takes mere minutes to make, and I can promise that it will taste 100 times fresher than anything out of a bottle. Just take either half of a good-sized seedless personal (mini) watermelon, or about 1/4 of a seedless standard watermelon, and cut the flesh into chunks. Pop the chunks into your blender, and let 'er rip on high, for two to three minutes, or until completely puréed. If you have a high-speed blender, you can simply go straight to making sorbet, but if your machine is a bit less thorough, you may be happier with the end results if you send the mix through a fine mesh strainer first. You will likely end up with a bit more juice than you need for this recipe, but that's the good news! It's absolutely delightful to drink all by itself.

Mango Colada Ice Cream

Makes About
1 Quart

Why should pineapples get to have all the fun? Make a splash by featuring mango in this tropical cocktail instead. For unbearably hot summer days, consider splashing this mix into the machine and drinking it as soon as it's done churning, as an adult slushy at its finest.

1 1/2 Cups Chopped, Ripe Mango
1/2 Cup Chopped Pineapple, Fresh
   or Frozen and Thawed

1/4 Cup Lime Juice
1 14-Ounce Can (1 3/4 Cups) Full-
   Fat Coconut Milk

2/3 Cup Granulated Sugar
1/3 Cup Dark Rum

Place all of the ingredients in the container of your blender, and purée until the fruits are broken down to a smooth consistency and the sugar has completely disappeared into the liquid. Strain if using a weaker blender, discarding the solids, and then chill the base in the fridge for two to three hours.

Churn in your ice cream machine according to the manufacturer's directions. Transfer the finished ice cream to an airtight container, and stash in your freezer for at least three hours before scooping and serving.

Marron Glacé Ice Cream

Makes
1–1 1/2 Quarts

The distinct scent of chestnuts roasting can instantly bring me back to the streets of New York City during the winter holidays; few other places still enjoy the tradition of hot chestnuts, readily available from dozens of food carts sprinkled throughout the streets. Enhanced with a whole vanilla bean but otherwise left to shine, the chestnut can finally make a grand entrance in something other than a metal cart on the sidewalk.

1 Cup Granulated Sugar
1 Cup Water
1 1/2 Cups Roasted and Shelled
    Chestnuts* (About 9 Ounces)
1 Whole Vanilla Bean, Split and
    Scraped

1/4 Teaspoon Salt
1/4 Teaspoon Ground Cinnamon
2 Tablespoons Non-Dairy Margarine
1 Cup Full-Fat Coconut Milk
2 Cups Plain, Non-Dairy Milk,
    Divided

2 Tablespoons Light Agave Nectar
2 Tablespoons Amaretto
1 Tablespoon Arrowroot

To candy the chestnuts, mix together the sugar and water in a medium saucepan so that all of the sugar is moistened, and then add the chestnuts, vanilla bean seeds, salt, and cinnamon. Cook over medium heat, and bring to boil. Once rapidly bubbling, reduce the heat to a simmer, and allow the mixture to stew gently for thirty minutes, stirring periodically, until the excess water has evaporated and thick, caramelized syrup remains. Add the margarine, and stir until it has melted in, coating the chestnuts evenly.

Remove half of the candied chestnuts to a clean plate and let cool. Returning your attention to the remainder on the stove, slowly pour the coconut milk and 1 3/4 cups of the non-dairy milk into the pan. Don't be alarmed if the sugar syrup crystallizes or seizes. Continue to stir, cooking gently, until the caramel dissolves into the liquid.

Separately whisk together the leftover 1/4 cup of non-dairy milk and arrowroot into a slurry before adding the mixture into the pan as well. Bring everything back up to a boil one more time. Simmer for an additional five minutes, turn off the heat, and let cool.

Transfer the thickened base to your blender along with the agave and amaretto, and purée until entirely smooth. Add in the other half of the chestnuts you set aside earlier, and lightly pulse to coarsely chop them, leaving a good bit of texture in the base. Chill thoroughly in the fridge for at least three hours before proceeding.

Churn in your ice cream maker according to the manufacturer's instructions, and transfer the soft ice cream to an airtight container. Let freeze solidly before serving, at least two to three hours.

*Roasting chestnuts at home can be a bit laborious, but not too tricky with a bit of know-how. Start with many more chestnuts than you'll need for the recipe because the shells add a good bit of weight, and, invariably, a number of them will prove less than edible once cracked open. One pound should be safe to start with, and if all goes well, you'll end up with a few to snack on in the end.

Preheat your oven to 400 degrees. Using a sharp knife, score an "x" into the rounded side of each chestnut, deep enough to go all the way through the shell and about halfway through the nutmeat, but not so far as to sever the quadrants. Place the chestnuts on a baking sheet and roast for thirty to forty minutes, stirring every fifteen minutes or so until the exteriors are lightly blackened in spots and the scored "x's" are beginning to peel away from the nutmeats. Let rest until just cool enough to handle, but be sure to peel them while still warm and pliable.

At this point the chestnuts will often still have a papery brown exterior, so to remove that, cover them in water in a medium saucepan, and boil for eight minutes. Drain, cool again, and peel away that final layer. You may find it useful to rub the chestnuts in a kitchen towel to loosen that final skin if it's giving you any grief.

Paradise Plum Ice Cream

Makes 1 Quart

Picture yourself sitting on a beach, hot sun beating down on your forehead, waves lapping at the sandy shoreline, lovely beverage in hand. Ordinarily, I'd be right there in that same fantasy too, but now that I've had paradise plum ice cream, that scene simply wouldn't be complete without a tall ice cream cone, rather than that paltry umbrella drink. All the best parts of a plum orchard and a tropical getaway meet in the middle, creating a little scoop of bliss.

2 Fresh, Ripe Plums (About 2 Cups Chopped)

1/2 Cup Chopped Pineapple, Fresh or Frozen and Thawed

3/4 Cup Granulated Sugar

1 Tablespoon Lemon Juice

1 14-Ounce Can (1 3/4 Cup) Full-Fat Coconut Milk

1/2 Cup Plain, Non-Dairy Milk

1 Tablespoon Cornstarch

Zest of 1 Orange

1/4 Teaspoon Ground Cardamom

1/4 Teaspoon Almond Extract

In a medium saucepan over medium-low heat, place the chopped plums, pineapple, sugar, and lemon juice, and stir well to combine. Stir every few minutes and allow the mixture to stew for about fifteem minutes, until the fruits have broken down to a thick, jam-like consistency. Mix in the coconut milk, and turn up the heat to medium.

Separately, whisk the non-dairy milk and cornstarch together into a slurry; then add to the saucepan. Bring the mixture up to a boil, and cook for an additional two minutes, stirring the whole time. Turn off the heat, and finally incorporate the orange zest, cardamom, and almond extract. Cool slightly before puréeing thoroughly in your blender, until perfectly smooth.

Chill completely in the fridge before churning the fruity custard in your ice cream machine according to the manufacturer's instructions. Transfer the finished but still-soft ice cream to an airtight container, and store in the freezer for at least three hours before scooping and serving.

Peach Melba Ice Cream

Makes About
1 Quart

Fit for an opera star, the original peach melba kept all components separate. The idea was that the warm fruits would bring up the temperature of the ice cream enough that it wouldn't threaten the precious vocal chords of Nellie Melba, Australian soprano of the late 19th century, and thus allow her to enjoy a frozen treat. Integrate all of those elements into one make-ahead dessert that merely needs to be scooped and served!

1 Pound Fresh, Ripe Peaches (About 3 Medium Peaches)
1 14-Ounce Can (1 3/4 Cups) Full-Fat Coconut Milk
1 Cup Granulated Sugar
1 Tablespoon Cornstarch

1 Tablespoon Arrowroot
Pinch Salt
1 Tablespoon Limoncello, or 1 Tablespoon Vodka + 1/2 Teaspoon Lemon Zest
1/2 Teaspoon Vanilla Extract

2/3 Cup Seedless Raspberry Jam
2 Tablespoons Water

First thing's first—pull out your blender, and add the peaches (pits removed), coconut milk, sugar, cornstarch, arrowroot, and salt to the container. Purée on high, until completely smooth; pass through a fine strainer to ensure there are no remaining pieces of unblended fruit in the final base, if using a lower-powered machine.

Pour the peach and coconut purée into a medium saucepan, and cook on the stove over medium heat. Stir often to make sure nothing sticks to the bottom of the pan, until the mixture comes to a boil. Cook for a minute longer; then remove from the heat. Add the limoncello and vanilla, stirring to incorporate.

Chill thoroughly in the fridge, at least three hours, before churning in your ice cream machine according to the manufacturer's directions. Meanwhile, microwave the jam for thirty seconds, just to loosen it up a bit without getting it too hot. Stir in the water, mixing until smooth and pourable.

Once finished but still soft, transfer scoops of the fresh ice cream to an airtight container, and drizzle some of the jam over each addition. Lightly stir everything together, to marble the jam throughout but not completely mix it in. Once the jam appears to have been distributed in approximately even ribbons, cover and store in the freezer. Let rest for at least four hours to further solidify before serving.

Pear-Cider Sorbet

Makes
1 Scant Quart

As soon as autumn leaves begin to fall, you can bet that our fridge will be fully stocked with at least a gallon of apple cider at all times. One of the few beverages that everyone enjoys, I can only imagine how many pounds of pressed apples we've drank. Stealing away a splash for this sorbet, I may have inadvertently stumbled upon an even more quickly vanishing form of apple cider. The soft flesh of pears adds a subtle creaminess to the sorbet, but rest assured, cider is the featured flavor here.

3 Medium-Sized, Ripe Bartlett or
    Anjou Pears (About 1 1/2 Pounds),
    Peeled, Cored, and Chopped

1 1/2 Cups Apple Cider
3/4 Cup Granulated Sugar
1 Teaspoon Lemon Juice

1/4 Teaspoon Ground Cinnamon
2 Tablespoons Grade-B Maple Syrup

Prep your pears, and place them in a bath of cider, sugar, lemon juice, and cinnamon, in a medium saucepan over medium-high heat. Bring to a boil quickly; then lower heat to maintain a steady simmer. Cook, stirring occasionally, until pears are fork-tender, about ten minutes. Purée the poached pear mixture in your blender until smooth. Stir in the maple syrup and chill for at least three hours before proceeding.

When mixture is cold, churn in your ice cream maker according to manufacturer's instructions. Transfer to an air-tight container, cover, and freeze for at least two hours or until ready to serve.

Pink Pomegranate Marble Ice Cream

Makes About
1 Quart

Making only a brief cameo appearance on the produce scene in November and December, the best way to get one's fill of pomegranate in such a short period of time is to utterly immerse yourself in it. Pomegranate ice cream with pomegranate ripple, topped off with pomegranate arils to serve if you so choose, is a very good place to start.

Pomegranate Syrup:

2 Cups 100% Pomegranate Juice
1/4 Cup Light Corn Syrup or Light
    Agave Nectar

Pomegranate Ice Cream:

1/2 Cup Full-Fat Coconut Milk
2 Cups Plain, Non-Dairy Milk
1 Cup 100% Pomegranate Juice
3/4 Cup Granulated Sugar

2 Tablespoons Cornstarch
1 Teaspoon Vanilla Extract
1/8 Teaspoon Peppermint Extract
    (Optional)
3 Tablespoons Beet Juice, for
    Coloring (Optional)

Prepare the syrup so that it can be cool and ready when it's time to churn the ice cream. Place the pomegranate juice in a small saucepan with the syrup, and boil over medium heat until reduced by three quarters; you should end up with about 1/2 cup total. This will take between ten to twenty minutes, so stay close by, and keep monitoring the progress. Cool, and then chill.

As for the ice cream base, whisk the coconut milk, non-dairy milk, pomegranate juice, sugar, and cornstarch together vigorously to beat out any lumps of starch that may form. Turn on the stove to medium heat, and whisk occasionally until the mixture reaches a rolling boil and has thickened significantly. Remove from the heat, cool completely, and stir in the vanilla extract. Incorporate the mint extract and/or beet juice if using.

Chill thoroughly before churning in your ice cream maker according to the manufacturer's instructions. Transfer about one-third of the soft ice cream to an airtight container, spreading it out to evenly fill the bottom, and drizzle one-third of the pomegranate syrup over it in a Pollock-like pattern. Repeat with another one-third of each, and then the remainder. Use a thin spatula or blunt knife to swirl the syrup throughout. Stash in the freezer until ready to serve. Consider topping scoops with whole pomegranate arils for some extra flair!

Raspberry-Mint Truffle Ice Cream

Makes
1 Scant Quart

Not just another raspberry and chocolate combination, this luscious assemblage combines fresh mint with tart, seedless raspberry purée, plus whole chocolate truffles. Due to their high cocoa content, they stay just as soft and luxurious after a trip to the deep freeze as other truffles would be at room temperature.

Raspberry-Mint Ice Cream:

1/2 Cup Fresh Mint Leaves, Packed
1 Cup Plain, Non-Dairy Milk
12 Ounces Raspberries, Fresh or
    Frozen and Thawed

1 Cup Light Agave Nectar

Chocolate Truffles:

6 Ounces (1 Cup) Semi-Sweet
    Chocolate Chips

1/3 Cup Plain, Non-Dairy Milk
1 Teaspoon Instant Coffee Powder
Pinch Salt

Starting with the ice cream base, roughly chop and bruise the fresh mint leaves; then combine them with the non-dairy milk in a medium saucepan. Turn up the stove to medium heat and scald the mixture (bring it just to the brink of boiling); then shut off the heat. Cover, and allow the mint to infuse for at least fifteen minutes. Strain out the used leaves, and discard them.

Once the minted "milk" has cooled a bit, pour it into your blender or food processor, along with the raspberries. Thoroughly purée, until as smooth as possible, and then strain once again, removing all of the seeds and pulp, and pressing hard to extract all of the liquid. Stir the agave into the seedless mixture, and move the ice cream base into your fridge, chilling for at least two hours before churning.

Meanwhile, prepare the truffles: place all of the truffle ingredients in a microwave-safe dish, and heat on high for just one minute. Stir vigorously, until all of the chips have melted and the mixture is entirely smooth and silky. If there are still a few stubborn pieces of chocolate that refuse to blend in, give the mixture another fifteen to forty-five seconds in the microwave, stirring well after each fifteen-second interval. Allow the liquid truffles to cool down to room temperature; then place the dish in the freezer to solidify.

After about one hour, take out the set but still-soft truffle mixture, and lay out a sheet pan lined with parchment paper or a silpat. Working quickly, scoop out very small balls of about 1 teaspoon each, and roll them lightly between your palms to make them at least mostly round. Perfection is not important here, and since these truffles are much softer than most and don't turn into chocolate rocks when frozen, they will become melty quite fast. It's a messy job for sure, but I wouldn't tell a soul if you wanted to lick your hands afterwards. Move the tray of rolled truffles back into the freezer, to wait until the ice cream is ready.

Once chilled, churn the raspberry base in your ice cream maker according to the manufacturer's instructions. As you scoop spoonfuls of the still-soft ice cream into an airtight container, layer each one with a handful of chocolate truffles, being careful that each ball maintains its shape as much as possible.

Let the ice cream cure in the freezer for at least three hours before serving, or until solid enough to scoop.

Rose Petal Ice Cream

Makes 1 Scant
Quart

Bright pink and *oh so* alluring, the rose-flavored gelato so ubiquitous in Italy held a special place in my heart—and stomach—long after returning home from that family vacation. Unfortunately, it was a fairly superficial attraction, owing mostly to that luscious hue and very little to the actual taste. Now it is time for this promising concept to finally prove its potential! This fine balance of delicate flowery essence and sweetness is the perfect combination of form and function.

1 Cup Organic, Unsprayed Rose
   Petals
2 Cups Plain Vegan Creamer

1/2 Cup Light Agave Nectar
2 Tablespoons Arrowroot
1 Teaspoon Vanilla Extract

1–2 Tablespoons Rose Water
1 Tablespoon Beet Juice (Optional,
   for Color)

Thoroughly rinse and dry your roses before beginning. It's better to be safe than sorry when dealing with flowers, because you never know if they may still contain dirt or bugs hidden between the petals.

Once perfectly clean, place the petals in a medium saucepan along with the creamer, agave, and arrowroot. Whisk well to make sure there are no lumps of the dry ingredients remaining; then place the pan over medium heat. Cook, whisking occasionally, until bubbles begin to break on the surface and the mixture is significantly thickened. Turn off the heat, and whisk in the vanilla, 1 tablespoon of the rose water, and beet juice. Cover and let steep for twenty minutes.

Strain out the rose petals using a fine mesh sieve, and discard the solids. Let the mixture chill thoroughly in the refrigerator, or for at least one hour.

Here's the important part—taste your mixture. Can you taste the roses? Is it flavorful enough for you? It should be just a touch too rosy, in fact, because the flavor will become slightly muted once frozen. If necessary, add rosewater until the taste is to your liking.

Churn in your ice cream maker according to the manufacturer's instructions. Transfer the soft ice cream into an air-tight container, and let rest in the freezer for at least three hours before serving, until solid enough to scoop.

Rum Raisinette Ice Cream

Makes About
1 Quart

Raisins seemed like some cruel joke, a poor substitute for candy back when Halloween rolled around. The only thing worse would be getting toothbrushes, but certainly there is no edible prize less appreciated by kids everywhere. So hide this one from the kids, because it's too good to share, anyway. Homemade chocolate-covered raisins perk up the standard rum raisin affair, because what isn't improved by a smattering of dark chocolate?

Rum Ice Cream:

3 Cups Plain, Non-Dairy Milk
2/3 Cup Granulated Sugar
2 Tablespoons Dark Brown Sugar,
    Firmly Packed
2 Tablespoons Cornstarch
1/2 Teaspoon Ground Cinnamon
Pinch Salt
1/3 Cup Dark Rum
1/2 Teaspoon Vanilla Extract

Chocolate-Covered Raisins:

2 Ounces (1/3 Cup) Semi-Sweet
    Chocolate Chips
1/2 Teaspoon Coconut Oil, Melted
2/3 Cups Raisins

Starting with the ice cream itself, combine the non-dairy milk, both sugars, cornstarch, cinnamon, and salt in a medium saucepan. Before turning on the heat, whisk vigorously to break up all lumps, big and small. Turn the flame up to medium, and whisk occasionally, until the mixture comes to a boil. Let cook at a full boil for two additional minutes; then remove the pan from the burner. Add in the rum and vanilla extract, stirring to incorporate.

Let cool to room temperature and then chill thoroughly for at least three hours before proceeding.

While the base chills, you can go ahead and prep the chocolate-covered raisins. Place the chocolate chips and coconut oil in a microwave-safe dish, and heat for approximately sixty seconds on full power. Stir well, but if the chips aren't entirely melted, return to the microwave and heat for an additional fifteen to thirty seconds, stirring again after each fifteen-second interval, until smooth. Add the raisins and stir to incorporate, coating the dried fruits thoroughly with the melted chocolate.

Pour your raisins onto a piece of parchment paper or a silpat laid out on a baking sheet, and spread out the clumps into individual raisins to the best of your ability. No need to go crazy and make sure they're all perfectly separated, but distribute them out into one even layer, none overlapping, at the very least. Place the baking sheet in your freezer, and let rest for about fifteen minutes, until the chocolate has solidified and is dry to the touch. Break apart any remaining clumps.

Once properly cooled, churn the rum ice cream base in your machine according to the manufacturer's directions. In the last five minutes of churning, slowly sprinkle in the chocolate-covered raisins so that the paddle of the machine incorporates and distributes the pieces throughout the ice cream. Transfer the soft ice cream to an airtight container, and store it in the freezer for another three hours minimum, or until frozen solid, before serving.

Short-Cut Spumoni Ice Cream

Makes
1 Scant Quart

Rather than laboriously churning each individual component of the traditional chocolate-cherry-pistachio trilogy, this rendition keeps things sweet and simple. A cherry base packed with dark chocolate chunks and toasted pistachios more than makes up for the lack of distinct, colorful stripes.

1 Cup Full-Fat Coconut Milk
3/4 Cup Granulated Sugar
2 Tablespoons Cornstarch
1/4 Teaspoon Salt

12 Ounces (3/4 Pound) Pitted Sweet
    Cherries, Fresh or Frozen and
    Thawed, Divided
1 Teaspoon Vanilla Extract
1/4 Teaspoon Almond Extract

1/3 Cup Roasted, Unsalted Shelled
    Pistachios
1/3 Cup (2 Ounces) Dark Chocolate
    Chunks or Chips

In a medium saucepan set over moderate heat, whisk together the coconut milk, sugar, cornstarch, and salt, beating the mixture vigorously to ensure that there are no residual lumps of starch. Allow the mixture to cook, whisking occasionally, until it reaches a gentle boil and feels significantly thickened in consistency. Take it off the heat and let cool for at least fifteen minutes before proceeding.

Measure 8 ounces (1/2 pound) of your cherries, and place them in your blender or food processor. Roughly chop the remaining 4 ounces (1/4 pound), and set them aside for the time being.

Pour the thickened coconut milk mixture into your blender or food processor along with the bulk of the cherries, and purée until completely smooth. Add in both extracts last, and pulse to incorporate. Transfer the cherry base into a bowl or pitcher, and chill in your refrigerator for at least two hours before churning.

Once the base is properly chilled, process it in your ice cream maker according to the manufacturer's instructions, adding the chopped cherries, pistachios, and chocolate chunks in the last five minutes or so of churning.

Transfer the soft ice cream into an airtight container, and let rest in the freezer for at least three hours before serving, until solid enough to scoop.

Sour Apple Sorbet

Green apples are generally a more tart variety than any red or yellow, but to call them sour would be a bit of a stretch. Compared to some of the sour candies on the market, which possess the astringent burn of battery acid, these mild-mannered fruits are merely a bit less sweet than their colorful cousins. That in itself creates a delightfully nuanced treat, but to really bring the pucker-power, you'll need the aid of citric acid.

1/2 Cup Fruity White Wine or 100% White Grape Juice
2/3 Cup 100% Apple Juice
2/3 Cup Granulated Sugar

1 Pound Granny Smith Apples (About 3 Medium Apples), Cored and Roughly Chopped (Unpeeled)
1/4 Teaspoon Salt

2 Tablespoons Lemon Juice
2 Tablespoons Light Corn Syrup or Light Agave Nectar
1/2 Teaspoon Citric Acid (Optional)

In a medium saucepan over moderate heat, combine all of the ingredients except for the citric acid. Stir well to combine, and bring to a boil. Reduce the heat so that you can sustain a gentle simmer, and poach the apples until fork-tender, about twenty to thirty minutes. Cool for at least fifteen minutes, purée in your blender to a perfectly smooth consistency, and strain through a fine mesh sieve if needed. Chill thoroughly before proceeding.

If using the citric acid, begin by incorporating just 1/4 teaspoon; then taste the mixture. If it's still not sour enough, go ahead and add the remaining 1/4 teaspoon. Be aware that it will likely become less pungent once frozen, so make the base just a hair more sour than you want it to taste in the end.

Churn in your ice cream maker according to the manufacturer's recommendations; then transfer the soft sorbet to an airtight container. Let rest and further harden in the freezer for at least four hours before serving.

Citric acid can be found in candy and baking supply stores, or in many pharmacies if you ask around. If you search your local grocery store's baking aisle, keep an eye out for "sour salt," which is another moniker for this ingredient.

Spring Blush Sorbet

**Makes About
1 Quart**

After a long, barren winter, the first green shoots that erupt through the ground come springtime seem like a miracle. Everything is new and alive again, and yet for months, there is hardly any fresh produce to be found. Fruits come so much later in the season than greens, but rhubarb, more a vegetable than a fruit, is the savior of many a spring dessert. Though bitter and virtually inedible raw, a little bit of sugar, zesty citrus, and berries does wonders for this early seasonal offering.

2 Cups Hulled and Quartered
    Strawberries, Fresh or Frozen and
    Thawed
1 3/4 Cups Chopped Fresh Rhubarb

1 Cup Granulated Sugar
1/2 Cup Orange Juice
1/2 Cup Water
2 Tablespoons Lemon Juice

1 Tablespoon Arrowroot
1 Teaspoon Vanilla Extract

Toss the prepped strawberries and rhubarb with the sugar to coat, and transfer to a medium saucepan. Turn on the heat to medium, and stir in the orange juice and water. Bring the liquid up to a boil and immediately reduce the heat to medium-low, to keep the mixture at a comfortable simmer. Stew the fruits for fifteen to twenty minutes, until the pieces of rhubarb have broken down and practically "melted" into the liquid.

Whisk the lemon juice and arrowroot into a thick slurry before incorporating it into the saucepan. Whisk thoroughly to distribute it throughout; then cook until the mixture comes back up to a steady bubble and has thickened a bit in texture. Turn off the heat, and cool slightly.

Blend lightly with immersion blender, or pulse the sorbet base briefly in food processor, but don't completely purée. You want to leave a bit of texture in this one, so don't strain out the remaining pieces, either.

Chill thoroughly for at least three hours before churning in your ice cream machine according to the manufacturer's instructions. Scoop the soft sorbet into an airtight container, and let rest in the freezer to further solidify, for at least three hours, before serving.

Sticky Date Ice Cream

Makes 1 Quart

Brace yourself for one serious sugar rush: gooey caramel topping mixed right into a date-infused frozen custard, this ice cream is true to the toffee-like cake that inspired it. Medjool dates are the gold standard, unfailingly soft, deeply flavorful, and as sweet as candy, but Deglet Noor are also an excellent alternative.

1 Cup Pitted Dates, Packed
2 1/2 Cups Plain, Non-Dairy Milk
1 1/2 Tablespoons Cornstarch
1/4 Cup Dark Brown Sugar, Firmly Packed

1/2 Teaspoon Ground Cinnamon
1/8 Teaspoon Salt
1 Tablespoon Non-Dairy Margarine
1 1/2 Teaspoons Vanilla Extract

1/4–1/3 Cup Butterscotch Sauce (page 196)

Roughly chop the dates before tossing them into a medium saucepan. Vigorously whisk together the non-dairy milk, cornstarch, brown sugar, cinnamon, and salt separately, double-checking that there are no clumps of starch before adding the mixture to the pan and turning on the heat to medium.

Bring the mixture up to a full boil, and then continue to cook, stirring constantly to prevent a spillover, for an additional two minutes, to allow the cornstarch to reach a fully thickened state. Turn off the heat, add in the margarine, and stir to allow the residual heat to melt and incorporate it.

Let cool for a few minutes, and then transfer the mixture to your blender. Blend it well, but leave a few small chunks of dates remaining for texture. Finally, mix in the vanilla, and chill thoroughly in the fridge, at least three hours.

Churn in your ice cream machine in accordance with the manufacturer's recommendations. Transfer scoops of the soft ice cream into an airtight container, smoothing out thin, even layers to cover the bottom of the container. Between each layer, drizzle a few thin stripes of the butterscotch sauce before covering with more ice cream. Use a wide spatula to slightly swirl all of the layers and sauce together, leaving a distinct ripple still intact but evenly distributed. Quickly move the container to the freezer, and let solidify for at least three hours before serving.

Strawberry-Lemon Curd Ice Cream

Makes
1 Scant Quart

Arguably perfect straight from the garden, it's tough to improve upon a whole, ripe, in-season strawberry. Of course, that won't stop me from trying! Adding a jolt of refreshingly tart citrus with a generous swirl of intense lemon curd serves to accentuate those fresh berries. A lighter, brighter choice that suits summer to the letter, a big bowlful can really hit the spot on a sweltering summer's day.

Lemon Curd:

3/4 Cups Granulated Sugar
2 1/2 Teaspoons (4.5 Grams) Agar
   Powder
1 1/4 Cups Lemon Juice
Zest of 1/2 Lemon

Strawberry Ice Cream:

1/2 Cup Granulated Sugar
1 1/2 Tablespoons Arrowroot
1 Pound Fresh Strawberries, Hulled
   and Roughly Chopped

1 Cup Plain, Non-Dairy Milk
1/2 Teaspoon Vanilla Extract
Pinch Salt

Start with the lemon curd so that it has plenty of time to cool and properly set up. Whisk together the sugar and agar powder to combine. Place the two into a medium saucepan along with the lemon juice and zest, and turn on the stove to medium heat. Whisk to break up any lumps of sugar, and continue whisking occasionally as it comes up to temperature. Once the mixture reaches a boil, turn off the heat and transfer the still-liquid curd to a heat-safe container. Allow it to come to room temperature before refrigerating until you're ready to use it. This step is very important, because tossing it in the fridge too early will weaken the gel, and you will end up with a runny filling. If, after a thorough chilling, the curd sets up too solidly and isn't spreadable, briefly run it through your food processor to break it down. Set aside.

For the ice cream, combine the sugar with the arrowroot in a medium saucepan, and toss in the strawberries. Pour in the non-dairy milk, stir to combine, and turn on the heat to medium. Bring to a boil, and then reduce to a simmer, stewing the berries gently for about fifteen minutes. Remove the pan from the heat, incorporate the vanilla and salt, and cool completely.

Chill in the fridge for at least three hours before transferring the mixture to your blender and thoroughly puréeing. I happen to like the texture that a few errant seeds will bring to this ice cream, but if you'd prefer your dessert perfectly smooth, strain the base and discard the solids.

Churn in your ice cream maker according to the manufacturer's instructions. Transfer spoonfuls of the soft ice cream to an airtight container, topping each addition of ice cream with a generous drizzle of the lemon curd. You may end up with more curd than you can use, but it does make up a big part of this flavor, so don't be afraid to lay it on thick in there. Once both components have been used up, take a wide spatula and swirl the entire contents of the container to distribute them evenly throughout.

Move the ice cream into the freezer, and let rest for at least four more hours before scooping and serving.

Superfood Fudge Ripple Ice Cream

Makes
1 Scant Quart

Ice cream may be just what the doctor ordered, at least when it's loaded with free radical-smashing antioxidants. Acai may be the latest craze in this department, but let's not forget that the more common assortment of berries and pomegranates still bring a lot to the table, too. Quickly whisk together a fudge syrup to swirl throughout the whole quart to sweeten the deal considerably, and you'll have some superfood medicine that's very easy to swallow.

Fudge Ripple:

1/4 Cup Light Agave Nectar
2 Tablespoons Water
1/4 Cup Dutch-Processed Cocoa
    Powder
1/2 Teaspoon Vanilla Extract
Pinch Salt

Acai Ice Cream:

7 Ounces (3/4 Cup + 2 Tablespoons)
    Unsweetened Acai Purée, Frozen
    and Thawed
1 Cup Fresh or Frozen and Thawed
    Blackberries
3/4 Cup Light Agave Nectar
1 14-Ounce Can (1 3/4 Cup) Full-
    Fat Coconut Milk
1/2 Cup 100% Pomegranate Juice
1/2 Cup Toasted Walnuts, Chopped
    (Optional)

Begin by prepping the fudge ripple: Whisk all of the ingredients very well, as the cocoa has a tendency to clump. It may be a bit tricky to incorporate, but just keep on stirring and everything will smooth out eventually. Place in a microwave-safe container, and heat for just one minute, to slightly thicken. Whisk thoroughly once more, and let cool. Set aside.

This ice cream could be considered "almost raw," and as such, requires no cooking and very little work at all. Simply blend all of the ingredients for the ice cream base, except for the walnuts, if using, and process until as smooth as possible. Pass the mixture through a fine mesh strainer to catch any remaining whole seeds, and discard those solids. Chill the base if not already cold.

Churn in your ice cream maker according to the manufacturer's instructions. Sprinkle in the walnuts, if using, in the last five minutes of churning. When finished, transfer to an airtight container in generous spoonfuls. In between each addition,

> If you're not a big fan of blackberries or don't typically keep them on hand, feel free to switch them out for any other sort of berry, such as raspberries or blueberries instead. Alternatively, a mixture of all of the above can work as well!

drizzle some of the fudge ripple mixture on top, until both components are finished. Lightly swirl a spatula through the whole quart to evenly distribute the fudge, but not completely mix it in.

Let the quart rest in the freezer for at least three hours to further set up before serving.

Thai Coconut Ice Cream

Makes
1–1 1/2 Quarts

The building blocks of Thai cuisine place their curries squarely in a whole separate category from other generic spicy stews. Spice intensities can range from child's play to heat that will burn holes straight through your esophagus, so I've learned to order with extreme caution when trying new Thai curry varieties. Always opting for flavorful spices over merely hot spices, both my sweet and savory recipes reflect that approach. Though this rich coconut custard does have a sharp hit of chili to it, the lemongrass, with its lightly floral, citrus aroma, is what really stands out in my memory.

1 Inch Fresh Ginger, Peeled and Chopped (About 1 1/2–2 Tablespoons Roughly Chopped)
1 Red Bird's Eye Chili, Seeded and Finely Chopped*

2 Stalks Fresh Lemongrass, Roughly Chopped and Bruised
Peel of 1/2 Lemon, Sliced into 4 Long Strips

1/2 Cup Unsweetened Coconut Flakes, Toasted
3/4 Cup Granulated Sugar
2 14-Ounce Cans (3 1/2 Cups Total) Full-Fat Coconut Milk

Prep the fresh produce, giving special attention to the lemongrass to extract the most flavor out of it. Lemongrass is very tough, so do your best to break it down into manageable pieces, and then crush it a bit to release the essential oils further. Combine everything else, including the sugar and coconut milk, in a medium saucepan over medium heat. Stir periodically as it comes up to temperature, until the mixture reaches a full boil. Turn off the heat immediately, cover, and let sit and infuse for at least one hour. Strain, and discard solids.

Chill for at least three hours before churning in your ice cream maker according to the manufacturer's recommendations. Transfer to an airtight container, and stash in the freezer for at least three hours before serving, to allow it to further solidify.

*Though less authentic to Thai cuisine, you could also use two to four jalapeños, one to two fresh cayenne or piquin chilies, or two to three chilies de arbol, should bird's eye be unavailable in your area. Just be sure to add spice to your taste, and remember that the flavors will become slightly muted once frozen.

Winter Mint Ice Cream

Makes 1 Generous
Quart

For those seeking something stronger than plain old peppermint, a pinch of white pepper gives this creamy concoction a bit of *oomph*. The mint is unmistakably the star, but without having an overinflated ego and becoming aggressive, grassy, or reminiscent of toothpaste. A fine line separates the herb from these qualities, but balanced with a good bit of agave sweetness and richness from both cashews and avocado, this is one vibrant, refreshing ice cream for all seasons.

2 Cups Plain, Non-Dairy Milk

1 Cup Raw Cashews

1 Ounce Fresh Peppermint Leaves

1 Ripe, Medium-Sized Avocado,
   Pitted

1 Tablespoon Lemon Juice

2 Tablespoons Crème de Menthe or
   Vodka

2/3 Cup Light Agave Nectar

2 Teaspoons Vanilla Extract

1/4 Teaspoon Salt

1/8 Teaspoon Ground White Pepper

It helps to have a high-speed blender to make this recipe, but you can also make do with a standard model; just be patient and allow extra time for your mixture to become completely smooth.

Simply place everything in your blender, and slowly increase the speed until you reach the highest setting. Pause to scrape down the sides of the container as needed to keep everything incorporated, and blend the mixture to a perfectly smooth, homogeneous purée. This will take approximately three to four minutes if using a high-speed blender. If you end up with small pieces of mint leaves visible, don't panic; it will still taste delicious. As long as the base itself is lump-free, it's better to stop mixing lest you risk overheating the mint and causing it to turn brown.

Chill the mixture for at least two hours before churning in your ice cream maker according to the manufacturer's instructions. Transfer the still-soft ice cream to an airtight container, and stash in the freezer for at least four hours to solidify before serving.

> Mint always seems to steal the spotlight away from the rest of the herb garden come dessert time, but basil is actually quite refreshing when paired with some sweetness as well. Try swapping out the mint for fresh basil leaves, and adding in 1/2 cup chocolate chips for a basil chocolate chip ice cream.

TOPPINGS, ACCOMPANIMENTS, AND COMPONENTS

Brownie Cookies

Makes 16–24
Brownies

Why not jazz up the same old ice cream sandwich, and make those cookies full-fledged thick and chewy brownies instead? Thinner than my usual approach but still with far more heft than a flimsy wafer, two of these chocolaty slabs make for a handheld dessert. Be sure to cut them fairly small, because, needless to say, they're very rich, and only more so when doubled and paired with a layer of ice cream in the middle.

6 Tablespoons Non-Dairy Margarine
1 Cup Granulated Sugar
8 Ounces (1 1/3 Cups) Semi-Sweet
   Chocolate Chips

3/4 Cup Vegan "Sour Cream"
1 Teaspoon Vanilla Extract
3 Tablespoons Dutch-Processed
   Cocoa Powder

1/2 Cup All-Purpose Flour
1/4 Teaspoon Baking Soda
1/2 Teaspoon Salt

Preheat your oven to 350 degrees and lightly grease a 13 x 9 baking dish.

Place your margarine in a medium saucepan over low heat, and allow it to melt slowly, so that it doesn't bubble up violently or begin to sputter. Add the sugar, bring to a steady simmer, and cook until the sugar has dissolved. Remove from heat and let sit for ten minutes. Mix in the chocolate, stir until melted by the residual heat, and add the "sour cream" and vanilla. Set aside.

In a medium bowl, sift together the cocoa powder, flour, baking soda, and salt before whisking them together to combine. Don't skip this step! It's critical to keep any lumps out of the batter and ensure that the dry goods are light and not packed together.

Add the wet ingredients into the dry; then stir with a wide spatula just until the mixture is smooth. Transfer the batter into your prepared baking dish, spread it out evenly, and smooth down the top. Bake for eighteen to twenty minutes, until no longer shiny on top and set around the edges. Do not be tempted to bake it any longer, even if it seems underdone. The insides should still be quite moist, so a toothpick test will not be helpful in this case.

Let cool completely, and for the cleanest cuts, chill thoroughly before slicing.

For tips on putting together picture-perfect ice cream sandwiches, see page xxiv of Essential Techniques, "Assembling Ice Cream Sandwiches"

Butterscotch Sauce

Makes 1–1 1/2
Cups

Often confused with caramel sauce, butterscotch is in fact distinctly different, as it gains its amber hue and sweet flavor not through caramelization, but by the use of brown sugar instead. This makes it an excellent sauce for those intimidated by boiling vats of sugar, and also a bit faster to complete.

1 Cup Dark Brown Sugar, Firmly
    Packed
1/4 Cup Light Corn Syrup or Brown
    Rice Syrup

1/4 Cup Non-Dairy Margarine
1 Teaspoon Apple Cider Vinegar
1/2 Teaspoon Salt

1/2 Cup Plain Vegan Creamer
1 1/2 Teaspoons Vanilla Extract

Place the brown sugar, syrup, and margarine in a medium saucepan, and set over low heat. Stir frequently until the margarine melts, fully moistening and incorporating all of the sugar. Turn up the heat to medium at that point, and let cook, undisturbed, for at least five minutes. Once the sugar has dissolved, carefully add in the vinegar, salt, and creamer, standing back as it may sputter a bit in protest.

Stir gently, and bring the mixture back to a simmer. Continue to let it bubble away for about ten to fifteen additional minutes, until completely smooth (not the least bit grainy) and slightly thickened in texture. It will continue to thicken as it cools though, so don't panic if it still seems a bit thin at this point. Turn off the heat, stir in the vanilla, and serve immediately or transfer the hot butterscotch sauce to glass jars. Let cool completely before sealing and storing in the fridge.

Sealed in an airtight container, butterscotch sauce will keep in the fridge for two to three weeks. To bring the sauce back to life, just microwave it at full power for thirty to sixty seconds before serving.

> Sometimes you feel like a nut . . . and sometimes you feel like having nutty butterscotch sauce—or, as I like to call it, "nutterscotch" sauce! Stir in 1/4 cup of creamy peanut butter after turning off the heat, mixing until smooth.

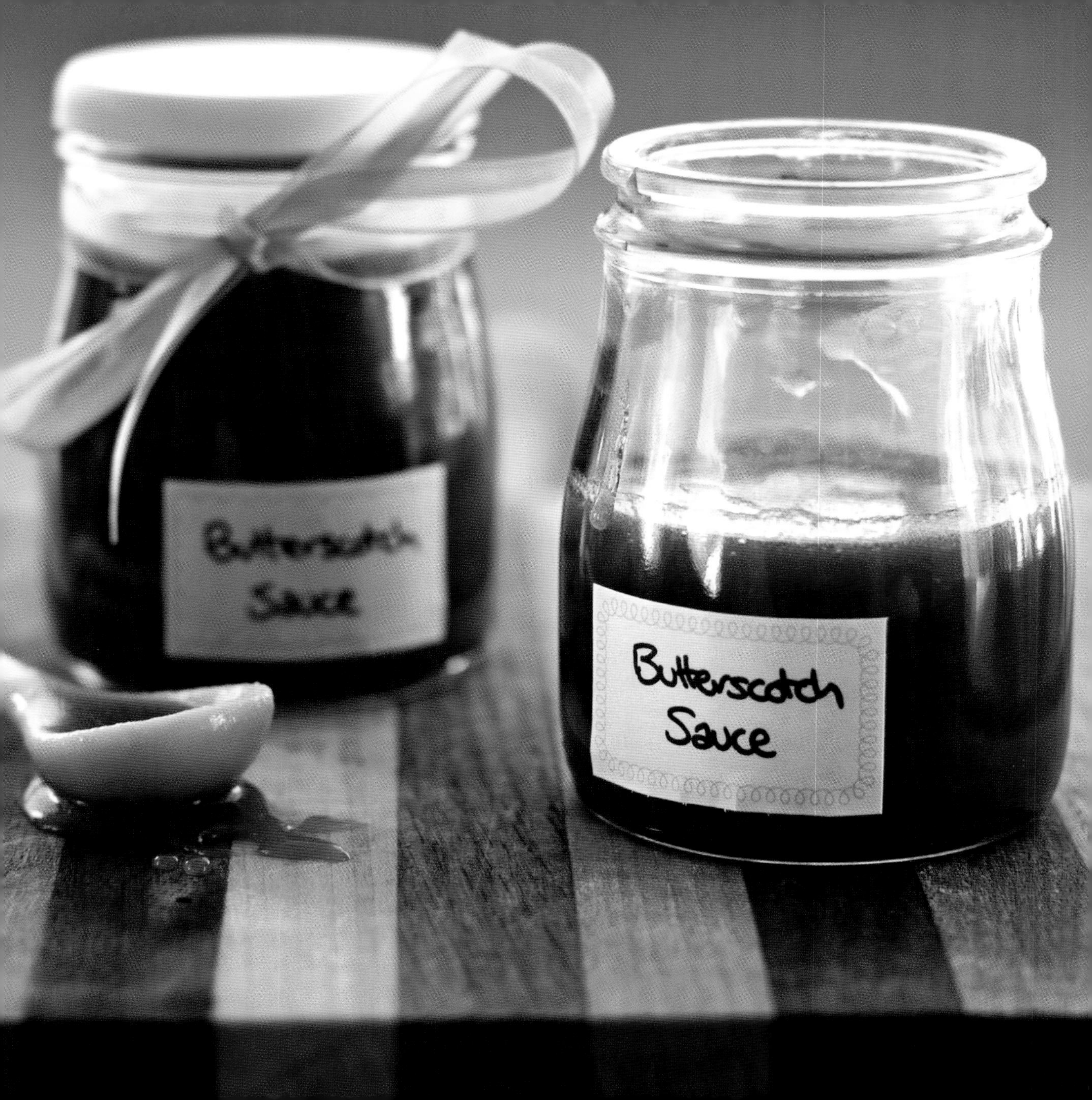
Butterscotch
Sauce
Butterscotch
Sauce

Buttery Rum Sauce

Makes 1 1/2–2
Cups

Best when bubbling madly and poured over icy desserts still frosted from the freezer, buttery rum sauce is a classic topping that may have lost popularity over the years, but is long overdue for a comeback. The contrasting temperatures make for a fast-melting but memorable grand finale to any meal. Boozy, uncomplicated, and incredibly satisfying, this is an adult ice cream topping that the kids will envy!

1/4 Cup Non-Dairy Margarine
3 Tablespoons All-Purpose Flour, or
　　Gluten-Free All-Purpose Flour
　　Blend

Pinch Salt
1/2 Cup Dark Brown Sugar, Firmly
　　Packed

1 Cup Plain, Non-Dairy Milk or
　　Vegan Creamer
1/3 Cup Dark Rum

This sauce starts out with a loose roux: melt the margarine in a medium saucepan over medium-low heat; then quickly whisk in the flour and salt, stirring vigorously to beat out any potential clumps. Stir frequently, lightly toasting the flour in order to remove that raw cereal flavor, for about five minutes. Be sure to continuously scrape the bottom of the pan, because it's prone to sticking and burning.

Mix in the brown sugar. Whisk constantly while slowly drizzling in the non-dairy milk, incorporating a little bit at a time and mixing until it smoothes out again. Once all the "milk" is in, turn up the heat to medium and bring the mixture to a boil. Remove from the heat when the bubbling becomes aggressive; the sauce should be significantly thicker in consistency.

Whisk in the rum, serve immediately or transfer to glass jars, and cool completely before sealing. Store in the fridge for up to two weeks. After chilling, the rum sauce is liable to thicken further, so you may want to thin it out with an additional 1/3–1/2 cup of non-dairy milk, returning it to a more pourable consistency. Whisk vigorously and microwave for thirty to sixty seconds before serving.

Gingersnap Cigars

Makes 12–16
Cigars

Putting the "snap" back into gingersnaps, these ultra-thin and crispy cookies are as much fun to make as they are to eat. Rolled into crunchy cigars, they're perfect to use as garnishes on ice cream sundaes or to simply pack into boxes and give as gifts. Should you feel particularly crafty, you can also drape the freshly baked disks over inverted muffin tins to form little edible bowls. The only thing that these spicy little numbers aren't is boring!

1/2 Cup Almond Meal
1/4 Cup All-Purpose Flour
1 Teaspoon Ground Ginger

1 Teaspoon Ground Cinnamon
1/4 Teaspoon Ground Allspice
1/4 Cup Non-Dairy Margarine

1/4 Cup Dark Brown Sugar, Firmly
  Packed
1/4 Cup Molasses

Preheat your oven to 375 degrees, and line a baking sheet with parchment paper or a silpat.

To begin, combine the almond meal, flour, and spices in a small bowl. Set aside.

Place a small saucepan over medium heat, and toss in the margarine, sugar, and molasses. Stirring occasionally, cook the mixture just until it comes up to a boil; then immediately remove from the heat. Pour the contents of your saucepan into the bowl of dry ingredients, stir to combine, and let the batter sit until it is cool enough to handle. About ten to fifteen minutes of chilling in the refrigerator should be fine.

Making only two cookies at a time, drop about one tablespoon of dough on the silpat for each cookie, placing them very far apart. These cookies spread *a lot*, and they will need your immediate attention when they come out of the oven, so even if it seems tedious to make two at a time, you will be thankful you did later! Bake for six to seven minutes, until bubbling all over and darkened around the edges. Pull the silpat or parchment paper off of the baking sheet as soon as it comes out of the oven, and let the cookies sit for just one minute. When they're cool enough to hold together when moved, begin carefully curling up one edge with your fingers, rolling it into a thin tube. Repeat with the second cookie. Reshape if they seem to bulge out in any spots, and let them sit with the seam sides down until completely cooled. They will continue to harden as they cool, and the final cookies will be pleasingly crisp and crunchy.

> Traditional gingerbread spices don't excite you? Switch it up and throw in a chai-inspired blend of 3/4 teaspoon ground cardamom, 3/4 teaspoon ground ginger, 1/2 teaspoon ground cinnamon, and a generous pinch of black pepper instead.

Golden Salted Caramel Sauce

Makes 1 3/4–2
Cups

Golden syrup is what truly sets this sticky topping apart. Bringing its inherently buttery, rich flavors to the party, it's like making caramel by starting with already caramelized sugar; half the work is already done for you, and the finished product will be twice as flavorful.

1/3 Cup Golden Syrup or Light Corn
    Syrup
1 1/4 Cups Granulated Sugar
1 Tablespoon Water

6 Tablespoons Non-Dairy Margarine
1/2 Cup Plain, Non-Dairy Milk or
    Vegan Creamer
2 Teaspoons Arrowroot

2 Teaspoons Vanilla Extract
1/2 Teaspoon Salt

Combine the golden syrup, sugar, and water in a medium saucepan and stir to combine. Turn on the heat to medium and continue mixing until the sugar begins to melt and dissolve. Take your spatula out and refrain from stirring again, to prevent gritty sugar crystals from developing. Swirling the pan occasionally to keep things moving, let the sugar bubble away until it turns deep amber in color, about fifteen minutes or so.

Meanwhile, whisk together the non-dairy milk and arrowroot, creating a loose slurry with no lumps. Set aside.

Once the hot sugar syrup has achieved a toasty brown coloring, immediately add in the margarine and "milk" mixture, standing back in case it splashes. The mixture may seize and look horrific, but with patience, it will come back together. Cook again over medium-low heat, swirling periodically, until the sauce is smooth and thickened. Turn off the heat and stir in the vanilla and salt. The consistency will be syrupy, but it will thicken more as it cools.

Serve while still warm, or transfer to a glass jar. Let it cool completely before placing the lid on the jar and stashing it in the fridge.

The caramel sauce will keep in the refrigerator for three to four weeks. Heat for thirty to sixty seconds in the microwave, and whisk it well before using.

> Caramel and apples are a match made in sweet tooth heaven. Bring this stellar duet together as an ice cream topping by switching out the non-dairy milk for apple cider or 100% unfiltered apple juice.

Graham Crackers

Makes About 30–40
Squares, or 15–20
Rectangles

Though my standard approach to super-crispy graham crackers has never failed me for countless pie crusts and tart shells, it doesn't translate quite as well to frozen desserts. Freezing to potentially tooth-cracking pieces, it was clear that a more forgiving texture was required.

1/2 Cup Non-Dairy Margarine
1 Cup Dark Brown Sugar, Firmly
    Packed
1 Cup Graham Flour*

1 1/4 Cups All-Purpose Flour
1/2 Teaspoon Baking Soda
1/2 Teaspoon Ground Cinnamon
1/4 Teaspoon Salt

1/4 Cup Amber Agave Nectar
1 Teaspoon Vanilla Extract

In your stand mixer, cream together the margarine and sugar thoroughly, until fluffy and homogeneous.

Separately, sift together both flours, baking soda, cinnamon, and salt. Start the mixer on low speed, and begin to gently incorporate the dry goods. Add in the agave and vanilla last, and continue mixing until the dough comes together, periodically scraping down the sides of the bowl with your spatula.

Once smooth, pat the dough out lightly into a flat round, and divide it in two. Wrap up each half in plastic wrap, and chill for at least two hours or overnight.

When you're ready to proceed, preheat your oven to 350 degrees, and line two baking sheets with parchment paper or silpats. Roll out one half of the dough at a time on a lightly floured, clean surface. Bring it down to about 1/8 to 1/4 inch in thickness, and use a fluted pastry wheel or plain pizza cutter to slice the shapes. Cut out your graham crackers into either 2 1/2-inch squares for ice cream sandwiches, or 2 1/2 x 5-inch rectangles to match the traditional cookie's dimensions. Carefully transfer the shapes with a flat spatula over to your prepared baking sheet and use a fork to evenly prick the cookies all over. Repeat with the second half of the dough. Afterward, gather up the scraps, re-roll, and repeat once more.

Bake for eleven to fourteen minutes for the squares, thirteen to sixteen minutes for the rectangles, or until very lightly golden brown around the edges and no longer shiny on top. Let cool completely on the sheets; then store in an airtight container at room temperature.

*A specialty blend of whole wheat flour, graham flour can still be a bit tricky to find, and has limited use beyond crackers. In a pinch, you can fabricate a close approximation of the wholesome flavor and coarse grind with 3/4 cup + 2 tablespoons whole wheat pastry flour and 2 tablespoons toasted wheat germ.

Hot, Hot Fudge Sauce

Makes 1 1/2–2
Cups

Some like it hot, but if you don't favor the spiced life, feel free to omit the cinnamon, cayenne, and chili powder for a pure chocolate fudge sauce. Even without the flavorful additions, it's plenty complex and of course decadent. Once chilled, it's thick enough to use as a spread, but reheats to an easily pourable consistency with just thirty to sixty seconds in the microwave.

2/3 Cup Plain, Non-Dairy Milk
1/4 Cup Confectioner's Sugar
1/4 Cup Dutch-Processed Cocoa
   Powder
1/2 Cup Light Corn Syrup or Brown
   Rice Syrup

1 Teaspoon Instant Coffee Powder
3/4–1 Teaspoon Chili Powder
3/4 Teaspoon Ground Cinnamon
Pinch Cayenne Pepper
Pinch Salt
2 Tablespoons Non-Dairy Margarine

6 Ounces (1 Cup) Bittersweet
   Chocolate, Finely Chopped
1 Teaspoon Vanilla Extract

Begin by combining the non-dairy milk, sugar, and cocoa in a medium-sized saucepan. Whisk vigorously and thoroughly, because these three will not play nicely without a fight. It takes a bit of elbow grease to incorporate the powders into the liquid, but keep at it until the mixture is lump-free. Afterward, add your syrup of choice, instant coffee, spices, and salt, whisking once more to incorporate.

Set the pan over medium heat, and whisk occasionally to prevent anything from sticking and burning on the bottom, until the mixture comes up to a rolling boil. Immediately move the pan off the heat, and introduce the margarine into the hot liquid, stirring gently to encourage it to melt in. Finally, add in all of the chocolate and vanilla, and whisk until silky-smooth. Let cool for ten to fifteen minutes before using, or store in an airtight jar in the fridge for up to a month.

Magical Shell

Makes About 1
Cup for Each
Flavor Variation

Textural contrast is what keeps a big bowl of ice cream interesting through each and every bite, and is precisely why a magical shell topping can be so dangerously addictive.

Chocolate Shell:

1/2 Cup Coconut Oil
3 Ounces (1/2 Cup) Semi-Sweet
    Chocolate Chips
1 Tablespoon Light Agave Nectar
Pinch Salt

Peanut Butter Shell:

1/2 Cup Coconut Oil
1/2 Cup Creamy Peanut Butter
1/3 Cup Confectioner's Sugar
1/2 Teaspoon Vanilla Extract
1/4 Teaspoon Salt

Vanilla Bean Shell:

1/3 Cup Coconut Oil
4 Ounces 100% Food-Grade Cocoa
    Butter
1/3 Cup Confectioner's Sugar
1/2 Whole Vanilla Bean, Split and
    Scraped, or 1 Teaspoon Vanilla
    Bean Paste
Pinch Salt

If you can operate a microwave, you can make your very own magical shell with ease. Simply place all of the ingredients for your chosen shell flavor into a microwave-safe bowl, and give it a blast at full power for sixty seconds. Stir well; if everything isn't completely melted and perfectly smooth, continue heating the mixture at intervals of twenty seconds, stirring thoroughly between each trip back to the microwave.

Let cool for at least ten minutes before pouring over your bowl of ice cream. Watch it solidify in a matter of seconds; then go ahead and shatter your handiwork!

Mellow Curry Powder

Makes About 1
1/2–1 3/4 Cup

Curry powders of all colors, flavors, and of course, levels of heat exist out there, unique to their own heritage and home cuisines. A naturally savory seasoning, picking out the perfect blend for a dessert can be tricky. For a store-bought blend, my go-to is always Madras curry, which is available everywhere spices are sold, is very mild, and complements nearly any food you pair it with. The absolute best option, however, is to make your own blend, suited to your personal tastes and guaranteed fresh. Courtesy of Sue Cadwell, chef and owner of *Health in a Hurry*, I'm thrilled to be able to finally share her secret formula.

1/2 Cup Ground Coriander
1/4 Cup Ground Cumin
2 Teaspoons Ground Cinnamon
1 Tablespoon + 1 Teaspoon Ground Caraway

1 Tablespoon + 1 Teaspoon Ground Fennel
1 Tablespoon + 1 Teaspoon Ground Black Pepper
1/4 Cup + 2 Teaspoons Turmeric

2 Tablespoons + 1 Teaspoon Ground Ginger
2 Tablespoons + 1/4 Teaspoon Cayenne Pepper

All you have to do is place your ground spices in a large glass jar, seal tightly, and shake until thoroughly mixed! In an airtight container, stored in a cool, dark place, this mixture should last for up to a year.

Mini Mochi Bites

Makes About 1 Cup

Having pounded rice to make mochi the proper way only once in my life, I'm perfectly happy to leave the "authentic" version to the masters. Anything that physical edges much too close to actual exercise for comfort, so count me out. Rather, my short-cut microwave version requires little more than stirring and waiting, making mochi effortless to whip up on a whim. Cut small into tiny bite-sized pieces, they're perfect for topping frozen yogurt.

1/2 Cup Mochiko*
1/2 Cup Confectioner's Sugar

1/2 Cup Water
1 Teaspoon Vanilla Extract

Cornstarch or Potato Starch, to Coat

Mix together the first four ingredients in a microwave-safe bowl, until mixture is smooth and free of lumps. Microwave on full power for two minutes, stir well, and microwave for another two minutes, until very thick and sticky like dough.

Scrape the hot rice dough out onto a clean surface very well covered with starch, to prevent sticking. Let it sit for about five minutes or until cool enough to handle. Sprinkle the top with additional starch, and knead lightly to smooth out the texture. Use a rolling pin to flatten the rice out to about 1/4–1/2 inch in thickness, and use a very sharp knife to cut bite-sized squares. If the knife becomes sticky, pause to wash it clean, and dry thoroughly before continuing.

Toss the exposed, cut edges in starch so that the pieces don't stick together, and eat at will. Mochi becomes progressively harder with age, so it's best when eaten on the same day, but it can be kept for three to four days when stored in an airtight container at room temperature.

*Mochiko is simply mochi flour, or glutinous rice flour. You can find this in any Asian specialty market or many sources online. Koda Farms® is one of the most common brands available in the United States; it can be purchased in compact, white 1-pound boxes.

To enjoy mochi as a stand-alone snack, toss the pieces in kinako (roasted soybean flour, also available at Asian specialty markets or wherever you purchase your mochiko) instead of starch, and top with a generous drizzle of kuromitsu. Meaning "black syrup," kuromitsu is traditionally made with unrefined Japanese black sugar, similar to dark muscavado, but you can also use treacle or mild molasses.

Pineapple-Ginger Sauce

Makes 1 1/2–1 3/4 Cups

Pineapples are steeped in symbolism, representing friendship, hospitality, and wealth. That also explains the origins of the traditional ice cream parlor pineapple topping—only the best accompaniments would do for a proper ice cream sundae, and sugary pineapple syrup was the height of indulgence.

We've come a long way, now that pineapples are available pretty much anywhere, anytime, and for relatively little money. That doesn't mean that the pineapple sauce of olden days must lose it specialness though. Updated with a burst of chewy candied ginger and a lighter hand on the sweetener, this simple sauce proves that the pineapple still deserves its title as the "king of fruits."

1 1/2 Cups Diced Pineapple, Fresh or Frozen and Thawed
1/4 Cup Finely Diced Crystallized Ginger
1/2 Cup Light Agave Nectar
1/4 Cup Lemon Juice
1 Teaspoon Arrowroot

In a medium saucepan, combine the pineapple, ginger, and agave, and begin cooking over medium-low heat. Bring up to a lively bubble; then keep the mixture at a steady simmer, stirring often, for around ten to fifteen minutes. The pineapple pieces should soften but not completely break down. Whisk the lemon juice and arrowroot together separately, breaking up any potential clumps, and pour the slurry into the saucepan. Continue to cook until the mixture comes back to a boil and the sauce has significantly thickened. Let cool for at least twenty minutes before serving, or store in a glass jar. Stored in the fridge, the sauce will keep for up to one week.

Rainbow Sprinkles

Almost more dear to my heart than the classic ice cream topping of hot fudge sauce, I was raised on rainbow sprinkles. Though plenty sweet, it took me quite a few years to readily admit that they had zero discernable flavor, let alone different flavors for each color. Regardless, the delightful texture and cheerful confetti appearance always kept us kids coming back for more. Making your own from scratch is a bit tedious, but for those looking for an edible project, with no chemicals or waxes, your patience will be rewarded.

Basic White Sprinkle:

1/2 Cup Confectioner's Sugar

1 1/2 Teaspoons Cornstarch
1/2 Teaspoon Vanilla, Almond, or Lemon Extract

2–3 Teaspoons Vodka

Sift the sugar and cornstarch together, being scrupulous about getting out any and all lumps. Add the extract of your choice, and slowly drizzle in the vodka, 1 teaspoon at a time, until the mixture becomes a smooth, very thick paste.

Transfer the sprinkle paste into a piping bag fitted with a very small, round tip. Pipe out long lines across either a silpat or piece of parchment paper, spanning the whole length of the surface. Let dry undisturbed in a cool place, for a full twenty-four hours, until dry to the touch and no longer shiny. Colored sprinkles made with liquids that replace any or all of the vodka (such as the red and blue) may take longer to fully harden, up to thirty-six to forty-eight hours, so be patient. Gently break the lines into short pieces, and store in an airtight container for up to three months.

Color Variations:

For each additional color, make a full batch of basic white sprinkles, and add the following:

Green: 1/4 Teaspoon Matcha or Spirulina Powder
Yellow: 1/8 Teaspoon Turmeric
Red: 2 Teaspoons Red Beet Juice Instead of 2 Teaspoons of the Vodka
Blue: 2 Teaspoons Natural Blue Dye* Instead of 2 Teaspoons of the Vodka

*Blue foods are rarely found in nature, and it can be a very difficult hue to re-create without some chemical aid. There are options though, and your best bet is to turn to the unassuming red cabbage. Finely chop half a head of red cabbage, and place it in a small saucepan. Add just enough water to submerge the pieces, cover with a lid, and simmer for one hour. Strain and cool, discarding the cabbage pieces or saving them for a stew later. You should end up with just an ounce or two of purple liquid. Use as is for purple coloring, or to reach the elusive shade of blue, add a tiny pinch of baking powder and stir well.

It's all a matter of science; red cabbage is very sensitive to pH changes, like an edible litmus test. Baking soda is alkaline, so it turns the extracted liquid blue. By contrast, vinegar or any other acidic ingredient would turn it red. Once the pH has been tweaked in either direction, the extract becomes much less stable and should be used within a few days to prevent the color from fading. It can't hold up to the heat of the oven either, so don't count on baking up blue cupcakes with this method.

Each individual batch will make approximately 1/3 cup of sprinkles; a full set of rainbow colors will make about 1 1/2–1 2/3 cups total.

Soft Ginger Cookies

Makes About 1 1/2
Dozen Cookies

Tender and chewy cookies with a kick of ginger, they're ideal for ice cream sandwiches, mix-ins, or solo snacks. This is my classic ginger cookie formula that makes an appearance every holiday season and has been the backbone of countless cookie platters. Though also quite popular with five-spice powder replacing the combination listed here, it's almost impossible to ruin such a fool-proof formula.

1/2 Cup Non-Dairy Margarine
2/3 Cup Granulated Sugar
2 Tablespoons Molasses
1 1/2 Cups All-Purpose Flour

1 1/2 Teaspoons Ground Ginger
3/4 Teaspoon Ground Cinnamon
1/4 Teaspoon Ground Cloves
1 Teaspoon Baking Soda

1/8 Teaspoon Salt
1 Tablespoon Water
1/4 Cup Turbinado Sugar

Preheat your oven to 350 degrees, and line a baking sheet with parchment paper or a silpat.

Install the paddle attachment on your stand mixer. Place the margarine in the bowl first, beating it briefly on low speed. This will soften it up a bit and make it easier to incorporate the dry goods. Add in the sugar and molasses, and cream thoroughly, pausing to scrape down the sides of the bowl as necessary. The mixture should be grainy but otherwise smooth, without any ribbons of unmixed molasses.

In a separate bowl, lightly whisk together the flour, spices, baking soda, and salt to combine. Add this flour mix into your stand mixer, followed by the water, and let the mixer do its thing. Be patient; it may take a few minutes for the dough to come together.

Pinch off 1–2 tablespoons of dough at a time, roll them into smooth balls in the palms of your hands, and then roll them each around in the turbinado sugar. Place the cookies spaced about 1 inch apart on your prepared baking sheet, and press down lightly to flatten out the tops. If the dough starts sticking to your hands, just lightly moisten them with cool water.

Bake the cookies for eight to twelve minutes; then let cool on sheets. If you prefer chewier cookies, bake for a shorter time; leave them in the oven longer for crunchier cookies.

Spiffy Whip

Makes About 2–4
Cups

Airy billows of snow-white whipped topping, sweet and simple, without any cloying flavors or unctuous richness—this is a lighter option, closer to the fluffy flourish topping sundaes straight out of my childhood memories. Though the ingredients at first may seem like the components of a chemistry kit, they're actually nowhere near as evil or fearsome as their names let on. Vegan protein isolates are simply pure protein, and are what create a fine matrix of bubbles here. The xanthan and guar gum, staples of gluten-free baking, simply hold that structure together. Isn't science sweet?

1 Tablespoon Wheat or Soy Protein
   Isolate
2 Tablespoons Granulated Sugar

1 Teaspoon Xanthan Gum
1/4 Teaspoon Guar Gum
1 Cup Plain, Non-Dairy Milk

2 Teaspoons Vanilla Extract
2 Teaspoons Lemon Juice

In a perfectly clean, dry bowl, mix together the protein powder, sugar, xanthan gum, and guar gum so that all of the components are evenly distributed; set aside for the time being.

Place the non-dairy milk in your stand mixer along with the vanilla, and install the whisk attachment. Start the mixer on medium-high speed. Very, very slowly, begin to sprinkle in the dry mixture, carefully aiming it right at the "milk" itself, not the sides of the bowl or the top of the beater. The gums will try to gel upon contact with liquid, so it's critical that the "milk" is constantly agitated during the entire time they're being incorporated.

The resulting liquid will be gooey, slimy, and generally repulsive at first. Do not panic!

Mix all ingredients together, and whip on medium for about two minutes. Add the lemon juice, and then turn the mixer up to medium-high speed for about seven to nine minutes, until light and fluffy.

Thin and Chewy Sandwich Cookies

Makes 8–10
Large Cookies

Like cookies and milk in a portable, frozen format, the idea to wedge scoops of ice cream between two soft, chewy chocolate chip cookies was a stroke of brilliance, and a pairing that has stood the test of time. They may not be my number one pick for all ice cream flavors, but with a few tweaks, the basic formula will serve you and your ice creams very well—literally.

1 Cup All-Purpose Flour
1 Tablespoon Cornstarch
1 Teaspoon Baking Powder
1/2 Teaspoon Salt

1/4 Cup Semi-Sweet Chocolate Chips
1/4 Cup Dark Brown Sugar, Firmly
    Packed
1/3 Cup Light Agave Nectar

1/4 Cup Margarine, Melted
1 Teaspoon Vanilla Extract

Preheat your oven to 350 degrees, and line a baking sheet with either parchment paper or a silpat.

In a medium bowl, whisk together the flour, cornstarch, baking powder, and salt so that all of the dry goods are evenly distributed throughout the mixture. Add in the chocolate chips and toss to coat.

Separately, combine the sugar, agave, melted margarine, and vanilla. Stir well; then add the wet ingredients into the bowl of dry. Using a wide spatula, mix just enough to bring the batter together smoothly without over-beating it. The batter may seem rather loose, but never fear, that means you're on the right track! Scoop out about 3 tablespoons of dough per cookie, and place them at least 1 1/2 inches apart on your prepared baking sheet. They spread out to become sizable cookies, so I usually bake about nine per sheet.

Flatten them slightly with lightly moistened hands, and bake for ten to twelve minutes, until barely browned around the edges and no longer shiny on top. They may appear to be slightly underdone, but they will continue to bake once removed

> For tips on putting together picture-perfect ice cream sandwiches, see page xxiv of Essential Techniques, "Assembling Ice Cream Sandwiches"

> For real chocoholics, create a Double Chocolate cookie by removing the cornstarch and adding 3 tablespoons of Dutch-processed cocoa powder instead.

from the oven, and you want to keep them nice and chewy. Let the cookies rest on the sheets for ten minutes before cooling completely on a wire rack.

Oatmeal Cookies go surprisingly well with ice cream, especially paired with sweet and simple flavors like French Vanilla (page 50) or Naked Frozen Yogurt (page 64). Just add 1/2 cup quick oats to the basic formula, and switch out the chocolate chips for raisins, if desired.

Tuile Ice Cream Cones

Makes About
20–24 Small Cones

Typical waffle cones are well beyond the reach of the average baker, requiring specialized equipment that can do one thing only: make thin and crispy wafers. Besides, waffle cones are a snap to find in any grocery store and are almost always vegan, no matter which brand you choose. Nope, tuile cones are a much better option for making at home. Easy to whip up in any oven, they demand only a bit of patience, as the baking process of tending to just a few at a time can be a bit slow.

1/2 Cup Non-Dairy Margarine
2/3 Cup Granulated Sugar
3/4 Cup All-Purpose Flour

1 Tablespoon Whole Flax Seeds,
   Finely Ground
2 Teaspoons Natural Cocoa Powder
1/4 Teaspoon Salt

Pinch Ground Nutmeg
1/4 Cup Water
3/4 Teaspoon Vanilla Extract

Preheat your oven to 325 degrees, and line two baking sheets with silpats. Parchment paper is not recommended, because it can ripple after numerous batches of cones and cause these delicate cookies to deform. You'll want to make a simple template to create even, round shapes, and you need an empty cereal box to do so. Cut out one of the large front or back panels from the box, and use a drafting compass to create a circle that's 5 inches in diameter. Cut out the circle, and voilà, there's your template! Set aside.

In your stand mixer, cream together the margarine and sugar until fluffy and homogeneous, pausing periodically to

Are you the lucky owner of a pizzelle or waffle cone maker? You can bypass all of the preheating and stenciling fuss and use it instead! Begin heating your pizzelle maker first, because the batter comes together very fast. Set out a wire rack to accommodate the finished wafers. Once you've assembled the batter as instructed above, very lightly grease each side of the pizzelle iron. I like to use a small cookie scoop to ensure even sizes of all of my wafers, but you can also just measure out about 2–3 teaspoons of batter per cone. Try placing it slightly off-center on the iron, just above the middle, because the action of pressing the top iron down tends to spread it outwards. After securing the lid (usually there's a latch, which I recommend employing for the thinnest, most even cones), bake for about thirty to sixty seconds, until golden brown. Quickly pry the cookies loose with a thin metal spatula, and shape as directed on page 221. Repeat with the remaining batter. You will likely get fewer cones with this method since each one takes more batter, but the resulting cones will be sturdier and less fragile than the tuiles.

scrape down the sides of the bowl as needed. Separately, whisk together the flour, ground flax, cocoa, salt, and nutmeg, distributing all of the dry goods equally throughout the mixture. Add the flour mix to your stand mixer, and turn it on to low speed to begin incorporating this newest addition. Pour in the water and vanilla last, and continue mixing just until the batter comes together smoothly.

Lay out your template on top of the silpat with the shiny, printed side up. This will help prevent it from becoming soggy immediately, but bear in mind that it's still a one-time use item, and will need to be discarded when you're done no matter how careful you are. Drop about 1–2 teaspoons of batter in the center of the open circle, and use a flat spatula to carefully spread out a very thin round, as thin as the template allows without leaving open holes anywhere. You may need to go back, add more batter, and smooth it out again. This takes some patience, but the right thickness is key to even baking. Place the template an inch or two away from the unbaked tuile, and repeat, but spread out no more than three tuiles per sheet.

Bake only one sheet of cookies at a time, until the edges are firm to the touch and are only barely, vaguely golden brown; seven to ten minutes. Working quickly, use a thin metal spatula to gently transfer one cookie to a flat surface. Carefully wrap the hot, flexible cookie around a waffle cone roller or metal cream horn mold, creating a cone shape. Place the cookie on a flat surface with the seam down, holding it closed, until cool and hardened. Slide the cone off the mold, and transfer to a wire rack. Repeat this process for the remaining cookies. If any become too cool and brittle for shaping, return them to the oven for thirty seconds or so to soften.

Repeat the baking and rolling process with the remaining dough. Tuile cookies are always best consumed on the day they're made, but will remain crisp for two to four days longer if kept in an airtight container in a cool place (but not the fridge; there's too much moisture in there).

Homemade cones almost always have holes at the bottom, varying from small pin-prick openings to rather gaping canyons. To prevent extreme drippage while eating your ice cream, plug up the bottom by filling it with a whole vegan marshmallow and/or melted chocolate, allowed to dry and harden.

Va'Nilla Wafers

Makes 24–36
Wafer Cookies

Stick with real vanilla, not "'nilla," to easily whip up a wafer cookie so good it could never have come out of a box.

1/2 Cup Granulated Sugar
1/4 Cup Dark Brown Sugar, Firmly
    Packed

1/4 Cup Non-Dairy Margarine,
    Softened
1/4 Cup Vegan "Cream Cheese"
1 1/3 Cups All-Purpose Flour

1/2 Teaspoon Baking Powder
1/4 Teaspoon Salt
2 Teaspoons Vanilla Extract

Preheat your oven to 325 degrees, and line two baking sheets with silpats or parchment paper. Set aside.

In your stand mixer, thoroughly cream together the margarine, "cream cheese," and both sugars, so that the mixture is fluffy and homogeneous. Scrape down the sides of the mixing bowl with a spatula as needed, to incorporate all of the ingredients.

Whisk together the flour, baking powder, and salt in a separate bowl before adding all of the dry goods into the stand mixer. Begin mixing on the lowest speed so that the flour doesn't fly out and dust the entire kitchen. Add in the vanilla last, and continue mixing until you've created a smooth, cohesive dough.

Scoop out about 2 teaspoons of dough per cookie, and roll into a ball between the palms of your hands. Place them at least 1 inch apart and flatten each ball out to about 1/4-inch thickness. Bake for sixteen to twenty minutes, until golden brown all over. Remove the silpats or parchment papers from the hot baking sheets and cool completely.

Store in an airtight container at room temperature for up to one week.

Vegan Honey-Flavored Syrup

Makes About 1 1/4
Cups

When plain old agave just won't do, this bee-free "honey" imposter is close enough to actual flower nectar that hive dwellers might confuse it with their own work. Even if you have no plans to use it in or on your ice cream, it's a delicious condiment to have on hand for tea, pancakes, or scones.

1 1/2 Cups Granulated Sugar
1/8 Teaspoon Alum (Optional)
1/2 Cup Water
1/4 Cup Amber Agave Nectar

1/2 Teaspoon Lemon Juice
1/3 Cup Dried, Untreated Rose
   Petals, or 1 Cup Fresh

1/4 Teaspoon Orange Blossom Water
1/4 Teaspoon Vanilla Extract

In a medium saucepan, combine the sugar, alum (if using), water, agave, and lemon juice, and bring to a boil. Reduce the heat so that the mixture maintains a gentle simmer for ten minutes.

Meanwhile, if using fresh rose petals, thoroughly rinse and dry them, being careful to remove any rotten or green sections.

Remove the pan from the stove and add in the rose petals. Stir to incorporate, cover, and let steep for forty-five to sixty minutes.

Strain out the spent petals (or just fish them out with a fork if they're easily removed) and finally mix in the orange blossom water and vanilla. Transfer to a glass jar and let cool completely before covering. Store in a dark place at room temperature.

The "honey" will keep almost indefinitely, but will begin to lose its delicate floral flavor after six months.

White Chocolate

Makes About 1–2 Bars, or 2 Ounces White Chocolate

Because this homemade version isn't tempered and lacks the typical stabilizers and emulsifiers of commercial chocolates, it doesn't hold up well to baking, but it's excellent melted or added to frozen desserts in chunks.

2 Ounces (1/4 Cup) Food-Grade
    Cocoa Butter
1 Teaspoon Vanilla Paste or Powder
1/4 Cup Confectioner's Sugar

1/2 Teaspoon Soy Milk Powder or
    Bird's Custard Powder
Pinch Salt

Have ready two chocolate bar molds, each measuring about 2 3/4 x 6 inches, or silicon ice cube trays of any shape; set aside.

Place your cocoa butter in a microwave-safe bowl, and zap it for just a minute or two, so that it liquefies. Be sure to keep an eye on it at all times, as it has a much lower melting point than a bar of finished chocolate. Once completely melted, quickly stir in the remaining ingredients, being thorough so as to break up any clumps of sugar and completely dissolve everything into the molten fat. Don't worry if it looks rather yellow at this stage, just pour everything into your molds, and it will be all right. Tap the molds on the counter lightly to remove any air bubbles, and don't even think about touching them again for the next few hours while they set up. I highly recommend parking them in the fridge to speed up the process . . . Just don't forget about them in there!

INDEX